W9-BFD-857

Frontiers in Health Policy Research 1

Frontiers in Health Policy Research 1

edited by
Alan M. Garber

National Bureau of Economic Research
Cambridge, Massachusetts

The MIT Press
Cambridge, Massachusetts
London, England

Send orders and business correspondence to:
The MIT Press
Five Cambridge Center
Cambridge, MA 02142

In the United Kingdom, continental Europe, and the Middle East and Africa, send orders and business correspondence to:
The MIT Press Ltd.
Fitzroy House, 11 Chenies Street
London WCIE 7ET
ENGLAND

ISSN: 1096-231X
ISBN: hardcover 0-262-07187-8
      paperback 0-262-57120-X

Copyright Information
Permission to photocopy articles for internal or personal use, or the internal or personal use of specific clients, is granted by the copyright owner for users registered with the Copyright Clearance Center (CCC) Transactional Reporting Service, provided that the fee of $10.00 per copy is paid directly to CCC, 222 Rosewood Drive, Danvers, MA 01923. The fee code for users of the Transactional Reporting Service is: 0892-8649/97 $10.00. For those organizations that have been granted a photocopy license with CCC, a separate system of payment has been arranged.

© 1998 by the National Bureau of Economic Research and the Massachusetts Institute of Technology.

This book was set in Palatino by Wellington Graphics.

Printed and bound in the United States of America.

National Bureau of Economic Research

Officers

John H. Biggs, *Chairman*
Carl F. Christ, *Vice Chairman*
Martin Feldstein, *President and Chief Executive Officer*
Gerald A. Polansky, *Treasurer*
Sam Parker, *Director of Finance and Corporate Secretary*
Susan Colligan, *Assistant Corporate Secretary*
Deborah Mankiw, *Assistant Corporate Secretary*

Directors at Large

Peter C. Aldrich
Elizabeth E. Bailey
John H. Biggs
Andrew Brimmer
Carl F. Christ
Don R. Conlan
Kathleen B. Cooper
George C. Eads
Martin Feldstein
Stephen Friedman
George Hatsopoulos
Karen N. Horn
Lawrence R. Klein
Leo Melamed
Merton H. Miller
Michael H. Moskow
Robert T. Parry
Peter G. Peterson
Richard N. Rosett
Bert Seidman
Kathleen P. Utgoff
Marina v. N. Whitman
John O. Wilson

Directors by University Appointment

George Akerlof, *California, Berkeley*
Jagdish Bhagwati, *Columbia*
William C. Brainard, *Yale*
Glen G. Cain, *Wisconsin*
Franklin Fisher, *Massachusetts Institute of Technology*
Saul H. Hymans, *Michigan*
Marjorie B. McElroy, *Duke*
Joel Mokyr, *Northwestern*
Andrew Postlewaite, *Pennsylvania*
Nathan Rosenberg, *Stanford*
Harold T. Shapiro, *Princeton*
Craig Swan, *Minnesota*
David B. Yoffie, *Harvard*
Arnold Zellner, *Chicago*

Directors by Appointment of Other Organizations

Marcel Boyer, *Canadian Economics Association*
Mark Drabenstott, *American Agricultural Economics Association*
William C. Dunkelberg, *National Association of Business Economists*
Gail D. Fosler, *The Conference Board*
A. Ronald Gallant, *American Statistical Association*
Robert S. Hamada, *American Finance Association*
Rudolph A. Oswald, *American Federation of Labor and Congress of Industrial Organizations*
Gerald A. Polansky, *American Institute of Certified Public Accountants*

John J. Siegfried, *American Economic Association*
Josh S. Weston, *Committee for Economic Development*
Gavin Wright, *Economic History Association*

Directors Emeriti
Moses Abramovitz
George T. Conklin, Jr.
Jean A. Crockett
Thomas D. Flynn
Franklin A. Lindsay
Paul W. McCracken
Geoffrey H. Moore
James J. O'Leary
Eli Shapiro

Since this volume is a record of conference proceedings, it has been exempted from the rules governing critical review of manuscripts by the Board of Directors of the National Bureau (resolution adopted 8 June 1948, as revised 21 November 1949 and 20 April 1968).

Contents

Acknowledgments

This series of meetings was initially proposed by Martin Feldstein, President of the National Bureau of Economic Research. He suggested that an annual health policy research conference held in Washington, D.C., would offer a unique opportunity to bring together academic economists and policymakers. He offered encouragement, support, and the resources needed to organize the meeting, and helped ensure its success.

I am grateful to the authors, each of whom worked hard to put together a paper and presentation that would be of special interest to a broad policy audience. I also thank the NBER administrative staff for their help in organizing the conference and publications; they include Sean Murphy, Richard Woodbury, Deborah Mankiw, Claire Gilchrist, Deborah Kiernan, Elizabeth Cary, and Kirsten Foss Davis. Finally, I am grateful to the National Institute on Aging, which has supported a large portion of the NBER's health care research agenda, and to the Commonwealth Fund, which supported the research reported in two of the chapters in this volume and helped defray the costs of this conference.

Introduction

This volume contains papers presented at "Frontiers in Health Policy Research," a conference held in Washington, D.C., on June 5, 1997. Convened by the National Bureau of Economic Research, the conference brought together academic economists who study issues of critical importance to health care policy and people whose expertise and interests are in the design and implementation of national policy— leading government officials, journalists, industry experts, researchers, and legislative staff. The conference was motivated by the belief that more extensive dialogue between the policy and academic communities would help make the work of the academic researchers more useful and relevant and that the results of their research could be helpful in assessing the consequences of alternative policies being considered in Washington and elsewhere. The conference is patterned after NBER's highly successful annual conference series, Tax Policy and the Economy, which began more than ten years ago and has been an important channel of communication between public finance researchers and tax policy experts.

The conference was held in a time of tumultuous changes in the organization of health care and its private financing. Perhaps the most striking change was the continued growth of managed care, which attracted substantial scrutiny and public concern about the impact of these changes on health care costs and on both the quality of and access to care. Did some groups suffer from denial of care, and did those that had access to care, such as the elderly, receive more limited and lower-quality services? Was managed care really saving money, or did it merely shift the burden of payment to patients and their families? The high rate of growth in the number of Medicare recipients choosing "risk contracts," or prepaid health service plans like those offered by health maintenance organizations, brought these issues to the federal government, particularly because Medicare represented one of the largest and most challenging federal entitlement programs.

After federal attempts to pass comprehensive health care reform bills failed, the private sector seemed to take the lead in transforming the market for health care. However, even though the initiatives were less sweeping than those debated earlier in the decade, federal interest in exploring ways to improve health care delivery and financing remained. In many respects, classic problems in health economics remained just as relevant for new reforms as for existing approaches to health policy. For example, adverse selection was a significant weakness of both proposed federal reforms and existing competitive insurance markets. Adverse selection occurs whenever insurance plans attract enrollees whose risk characteristics—and expected claims—deviate significantly from averages for the population. Health insurance plans that are more attractive to "high-risk" enrollees have predictably higher utilization of health care and therefore higher expenditures. Thus any increase in revenues from the premiums such plans attract is usually less than the added costs they bear when they enroll high-risk individuals. The consequences of adverse selection may be as severe as the collapse of health insurance markets, or more likely, the redesign of insurance plans to minimize its impact.

Although this phenomenon is ordinarily considered most important in private insurance markets, adverse selection may also have been the most important drawback to the proposal to allow Medicare recipients to participate in medical savings accounts (MSAs). MSAs consist of tax-advantaged savings accounts intended to pay for all but catastrophic health expenditures. Because participation in MSAs would have been optional, allowing Medicare recipients to choose freely between traditional Medicare and a plan that provided catastrophic insurance with the savings plan, there were fears that healthy Medicare recipients would choose MSAs, whereas those who used Medicare-financed services heavily would stay in the traditional plan. The loss of the low-risk enrollees would greatly raise the average costs of the traditional program.

Because adverse selection is a pervasive problem for health insurance, it is grist for the health economist's mill. Yet the literature on this subject proposes few fully satisfactory solutions. Despite the lack of ideal solutions, policymakers who ignore adverse selection do so at their peril. This theme emerges from the study by David Cutler and Richard Zeckhauser on risk sorting across health insurance plans. They explain the phenomenon in particularly lucid terms, examining its consequences in two large groups of Massachusetts employees. They present a clear taxonomy of the types of losses adverse selection induces, which include mismatching between enrollees and health insurance plans, viatiation of some of insurance's risk-reducing properties, and inefficient characteristics that health insurance policies must incorporate to reduce adverse selection. Some of their findings are unexpected and intriguing. For example, many employers now attempt to equalize the employer contribution to health insurance plans offered to their employees, so that employees who choose high-cost plans must pay the added premiums themselves. At Harvard University, one of the employers studied, the implementation of equal employer contributions resulted in the disappearance of the most generous health insurance policy in less than three years. The other group studied, the Group Insurance Commission of Massachusetts, sustained the most generous policy it offered by subsidizing it and directly managing its costs. These findings highlight the frequent observation that the presence of health insurance and its peculiar characteristics often means that the application of straightforward, well-accepted economic principles in the context of market failures induced by health insurance can lead to unanticipated, undesirable outcomes.

Because they suffer disproportionately from chronic diseases, the elderly are particularly heavy users of health care. Consequently they may have much to gain—or lose—with changes in health care markets. In many respects, the elderly are the best-insured Americans. Nearly all have hospital insurance under Medicare Part A, and the overwhelming majority have coverage for physicians' services under Medicare Part B. Nevertheless, Medicare coverage has large gaps. For example, elderly Americans who lack supplemental private insurance must bear the cost of prescription drugs themselves, because Medicare does not pay for them. For many of the elderly, such drugs represent a very large out-of-pocket expense. Thus it is natural to ask whether changes in the market for drugs—such as the introduction of new drugs and changes in the prices of existing drugs—have imposed a particularly onerous economic burden on the elderly.

Determining the prices that are paid for drugs at either the wholesale or retail level, and even constructing a price index for drugs, require a number of judgments about changes in the mix of drugs that people use and which set of prices to apply. As part of a general research effort to understand changes in the price and quality of drugs over time, Ernst Berndt and colleagues examined whether changes in the price of prescription drugs over time disproportionately affected the elderly. They posit two alternative hypotheses about how the elderly would be affected.

First, the elderly may be considered more fragile, and therefore preferentially receive newer treatments that are more convenient to use and less likely to cause side effects or interactions with other drugs. Thus the elderly would be more likely to receive newer, branded drugs; if price inflation is greater for these products, the elderly would experience more rapid increases in drug costs than the young. A second hypothesis recognizes that the elderly often continue to use the same drug for many years, particularly if it is working well. If this effect predominates, the elderly would disproportionately use older drugs, often available in generic form, whose prices tend to rise less rapidly than branded drugs. Then their rate of price inflation would be less than for the young.

Using sophisticated methodology and a unique set of data on prescription pharmaceutical sales and pricing from 1990 to 1996, Berndt and colleagues find support for both hypotheses but for different drug classes. Price inflation in antibiotics used by the elderly was greater than for those used by the young, in part because the elderly tended to use newer drug formulations that had fewer side effects. On the other hand, the elderly tended to use older, less-expensive antidepressants than the young, resulting in a lower than average rate of inflation for the elderly than for the young treated with this class of drugs. For calcium channel blockers, used primarily to treat hypertension and angina pectoris, there was no significant difference in the rate of growth of prices in drugs used by the elderly or the young. These results suggest that overall the elderly are not subject to greater inflation in drug cost than the young, although the elderly who lack supplemental insurance and live on fixed incomes may be more vulnerable than the young to the financial cost associated with drug price rises.

One of the forces expected to moderate expenditure growth is the change in the way that Americans receive their health care. More and more are enrolling in managed-care plans, which incorporate a variety of features to limit health care utilization and control costs. Many managed-care plans pay providers on a completely or partially capitated basis, meaning that some or all health services are provided for a fixed fee paid either annually or monthly. The incentives implicit in most managed-care plans offer the hope that costs can be controlled and stimulate fears that effective care will be denied and the quality of health services will decline. Two chapters address how managed care has influenced the growth of health expenditures. One, by Cutler and Louise Sheiner, examines cross-state data to assess how the expansion of managed care influenced the growth of medical expenditures generally; the other, by Laurence Baker and Sharmila Shakarkumar, looks at similar issues specifically for Medicare. Cutler and Sheiner find that in states in which managed-care enrollment increased, the rate of cost growth for hospital care slowed. Although states with more managed care tended also to experience greater growth in spending for physicians' services, the decline in hospital expenditures more than offset this growth. Their results challenge the traditional view of HMOs' effect on health care costs. Evidence obtained from two decades ago suggests that HMOs achieve substantial savings compared to fee-for-service plans, largely by reducing hospital utilization. But the rate of growth of expenditures, according to the traditional view, is the same for HMOs and other health care financing plans. This implies that a switch from fee-for-service to HMOs will produce only transient savings, because the growth in expenditures will make HMO costs reach the levels of fee-for-service in a few years. Cutler and Sheiner's work, in contrast, indicates that managed care may indeed dampen medical expenditure growth by slowing the adoption of new technologies, so that managed care may have far more significant effects on long-term expenditure growth than previous studies suggested.

The Baker and Shankarkumar study emphasizes the importance of "spillover effects," the effects of managed-care penetration on the economic behavior of non–managed-care providers. In particular, they hypothesize that greater competition introduced by managed care may cause providers, even those reimbursed on a traditional fee-for-service basis, to lower prices or change the type or intensity of the care they provide. If such effects occur, typical estimates of the overall effects of managed care on health expenditures may be too small. To investigate this issue, Baker and Shankarkumar explore geographic variation in HMO market share and expenditures for Medicare beneficiaries enrolled in the traditional fee-for-service plans. They find that managed care's penetration in the local health care market, for both Medicare and non-Medicare recipients, is associated with declines in both Part A and Part B fee-for-service expenditures. Notably, this effect does not specifically reflect the percentage of Medicare recipients in an area who enroll in managed-care plans. Increases in the Medicare HMO market share, as opposed to the overall HMO market share, are associated with increases in Part A expenditures and with only small decreases in Part B expenditures. This study strongly supports the view that managed care has effects on health care delivery and pricing that extend well beyond enrollees in managed-care plans.

Health insurance, whether provided by government or the private sector, has an important role in protecting the most vulnerable populations, such as patients with chronic illnesses or severe acute illnesses that result in very high expenditures. Changes in health care financing that allow greater choice may paradoxically disadvantage such individuals. Choice can affect them adversely because it can interfere with their ability to benefit from wider pooling of risk; individuals who expect to have lower than average expenditures will tend to choose plans that cost less or provide a more attractive bundle of services, whereas plans with higher premiums and more comprehensive coverage for serious illnesses or a wider choice of providers tend to attract an increasingly high-risk group of enrollees. Eventually, the comprehensive, expensive health insurance plans may cease to exist because their costs, and premiums, become prohibitive as they attract an increasingly high-risk group of subscribers. This form of adverse selection is most likely when high expenditures are predictable. The distribution of health expenditures, both for Medicare and for the general population, suggests that individuals differ greatly in their health care consumption, so adverse selection is likely to be a major problem.

It is well known, for example, that a small proportion of all Medicare recipients account for a greatly disproportionate share of program expenditures. Much of what is known, however, is based on single years or single episodes of care. Is it possible to identify a population of patients who can be expected to have very high costs of health care year after year? One factor that would mitigate any such effects is the high mortality rate associated with high expenditures. Medicare recipients in the last year of life, for example, consume much more health care than the average Medicare recipient, adjusted for age and sex. If many or most of the very high-cost Medicare recipients die, high expenditures should not persist from one year to the next. The paper by my colleagues Thomas MaCurdy, Mark McClellan, and me investigates skewness in expenditures both within a year and across many years to gain insights into the predictability of high expenditures and the likelihood that adverse selection would be a problem over a long time period. We find that, from 1987 to 1995, high-cost users were responsible for much of the growth of Medicare's hospital payments. However, payments for physician services grew mainly because more beneficiaries used the services. Very few Medicare beneficiaries remain in the highest cost categories for multiple years, limiting the magnitude of expenditure persistence, but we find that high expenditures are sufficiently persistent to pose major adverse-selection problems. Any policy reform will need to recognize this characteristic of Medicare expenditures.

Like other ongoing work of NBER's Program in Health Care, the studies reported here are intended to offer new information and perspectives on key health policy issues to inform discussions about possible solutions to existing and future problems in health care financing and delivery. We hope that these contributions will stimulate further dialogue and ultimately advance the development of innovative solutions to health policy problems.

1

Adverse Selection in Health Insurance

David M. Cutler and Richard J. Zeckhauser
Harvard University and National Bureau of Economic Research

Executive Summary

Individual choice among health insurance policies may result in risk-based sorting across plans. Such adverse selection induces three types of losses: efficiency losses from individuals' being allocated to the wrong plans; risk-sharing losses, because premium variability is increased; and losses from insurers' distorting their policies to improve their mix of insureds. We discuss the potential for these losses and present empirical evidence on adverse selection in two groups of employees: Harvard University and the Group Insurance Commission of Massachusetts (serving state and local employees). In both groups, adverse selection is a significant concern. Harvard's decision to contribute an equal amount to all insurance plans led to the disappearance of the most generous policy within three years. The Group Insurance Commission has contained adverse selection by subsidizing premiums proportionally and managing the most generous policy very tightly. A combination of prospective or retrospective risk adjustment, coupled with reinsurance for high-cost cases, seems promising as a way to provide appropriate incentives for enrollees and to reduce losses from adverse selection.

Individuals who expect high health care costs differentially prefer more generous and expensive insurance plans; those who expect low costs choose more moderate plans. This phenomenon, called adverse selection, is a major theoretical concern in health insurance markets.

This paper was prepared for the National Bureau of Economic Research conference on Frontiers in Health Policy Research, June 5, 1997.

David M. Cutler is Professor of Economics, Harvard University, and Research Associate, National Bureau of Economic Research. Richard J. Zeckhauser is Frank Plumpton Ramsey Professor of Political Economy, Kennedy School of Government, Harvard University, and Research Associate, National Bureau of Economic Research.

We are grateful to Dan Altman and Srikanth Kadiyala for assistance, and to Sarah Reber, Charles Slavin, and Miriam Avins for helpful discussions. This work was supported by a grant from the National Institutes on Aging to NBER as well as from TIAA to Harvard.

Adverse selection can lead to three classes of inefficiencies: Prices to participants do not reflect marginal costs, hence on a benefit-cost basis individuals select the wrong health plans; desirable risk spreading is lost; and health plans manipulate their offerings to deter the sick and attract the healthy.

Discussions of health care reform have often become stuck over the issue of adverse selection. Concerns about adverse selection have been raised in the context of Medicare reform, changes in employment-based health insurance, and the efficiency of individual insurance markets (see Cutler 1996 for discussion). But how important are these concerns empirically? Should we be greatly worried about adverse selection or consider it a minor issue? What measures might mitigate its effects?

We address these issues in this chapter, focusing in particular on individuals' choice of a health insurance plan from a menu set by their employer. We draw heavily on case studies of two entities for which we have detailed information that enables us to assess the importance of adverse selection: Harvard University and the Group Insurance Commission of Massachusetts. We conclude that adverse selection is a real and growing issue in a world where most employers offer multiple alternative insurance policies. Adverse selection eliminated the market for a generous preferred provider organization at Harvard and threatens to do the same with a generous indemnity policy at the Group Insurance Commission, absent measures to diminish adverse selection.

We begin the chapter with a discussion of adverse selection. We then consider the empirical importance of this phenomenon, using data from our two examples. Finally, we discuss strategies—including mandatory reinsurance and payment adjustments to plans that enroll high risks—to mitigate the effects of adverse selection.

I. The Theory of Adverse Selection

We illustrate the issues involved in adverse selection by considering employer-administered health plans, although the issues could just as well apply to government-sponsored insurance or individuals purchasing insurance on their own. (The original treatment of adverse selection is Rothschild and Stiglitz 1976.) Typically, employers offer individuals multiple health plans to promote competition and to cater to individual tastes in styles of medical care delivery and choice of medical providers.

When employers set out multiple insurance offerings and allow insurers flexibility in designing their plans, high-risk individuals may differentially choose some plans and low risks another. We label this process differential selection. When differential selection occurs because individuals are not charged marginal cost when choosing among plans, it is called adverse selection, and it has implications for efficiency.

Three parties play a role in differential selection. Insurers set premiums on the basis of the riskiness of the people they enroll and their negotiations with employers. Employers pay some portion of the premiums and require some contribution by employees. Employees choose a health care plan based on a benefit-cost calculation—those who believe they are likely to need more care buy the more expensive policy—as well as preferences, such as the plan's geographic locations, whether they can continue to see doctors with whom they have already established relationships, or whether friends recommend the plan. If such preferences exert sufficient influence, risk-based selection is a minor consideration; as they become less important, adverse selection increases.

Figure 1.1 shows how the confluence of actions by insurers, employers, and employees produces an outcome yielding plan premiums, employee charges, and an allocation of people to plans. This process can lead to inefficient allocation of employees across plans, incomplete risk spreading, and perverse incentives for plans to attract particular employees differentially, as we now show.

Adverse Selection and Inefficient Allocation: An Example   We illustrate the adverse-selection process with a simple hypothetical example. An employer offers two health plans, a generous plan and a moderate plan. We also assume two types of individuals—high risk and low risk. The costs for treating individuals under the plans, and their gains in benefit from the generous plan, are

| | Resource costs of coverage | | | Benefit difference: generous less moderate plan |
	Moderate	Generous	Difference	
Low-risk individuals	$40	$60	$20	$15
High-risk individuals	70	100	30	40

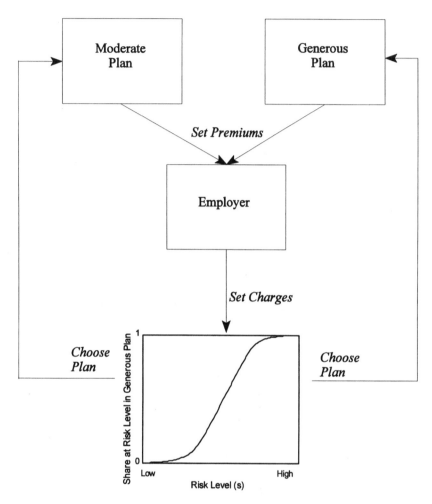

Figure 1.1
Differential selection: Plan, employer, and employee actions

High risks are more expensive than low risks, and spending is greater under the generous plan for each risk type. The last column shows the posited gain in benefits the different types of individuals receive from the generous as opposed to the moderate plan. It is assumed that high risks benefit more than low risks from increased plan generosity.

The efficient outcome in this example is for high-risk people to be in the more generous plan and low risk people to be in the moderate plan. High risks should be in the generous plan because the incremental value of that plan to them ($40) is greater than its additional cost ($30). For low risks, the opposite is true ($15 < $20).

We suppose that insurers charge the same premium for everyone enrolled in the plan, possibly because individuals are indistinguishable to the insurer, equal premiums are required by law, or employers adopt this policy to help spread risks.[1] Starting at the efficient equilibrium, the premiums that would cover costs in this case are $40 for the moderate plan and $100 for the generous plan. If these premiums were offered, however, all of the high-risk people would switch to the low-risk plan: the additional cost to high risks of the more generous plan ($60) is not worth the additional benefit ($40). Thus, everyone would wind up in the moderate plan. The reason is simple: A person who switches from the generous to moderate plan benefits by mixing in with lower-risk individuals, and since premiums reflect risk mixes, this distorts choices towards the moderate plan.

A More Complete Model   We now examine adverse selection in a more realistic framework. As before, the employer offers two health insurance plans, generous and moderate. The generous plan may offer a greater choice of providers, lower cost sharing, or less officious gatekeepers than the moderate plan. The generous policy might be a fee-for-service (FFS) indemnity policy or a preferred provider organization (PPO), whereas the moderate policy might be a health maintenance organization (HMO). For the moment, we take the characteristics of the two policies as fixed and focus on the employer's most important decision: What portion of the premium should he pay, and what portion should be charged to the employee?

---

1. Even if insurance premiums do vary across insureds, they may not fully reflect the cost differences that individuals know they are likely to experience.

Three decades ago, many employers offered just one health plan. Those who offered more than one plan frequently charged employees the same amount for each, subsidizing whatever difference there was between what employees paid and the premiums the plans charged the employer. The dollar amounts were not great, and the subsidy was tax advantaged, being deductible to the employer but not taxed to the employee.

Since then, health care costs have escalated and marginal personal tax rates have declined, making subsidies to health insurance less attractive. Employers have responded by reducing subsidies to health insurance. They have also sought to set employee charges for the different plans that would make their employees face appropriate incentives when choosing among the plans, which can now differ substantially in cost. A common practice is to offer the same dollar subsidy whichever plan is chosen, the so-called equal contribution rule. Other employers subsidize a fixed percentage of each plan's costs. The question that we ask is how these two pricing strategies affect outcomes. For expositional ease, we label as "premium" the per employee amount that plans charge for enrollment, "contribution" what the employer pays toward the premium, and "charge" the amount that the employer requires an employee to pay to enroll in a plan.

We assume employees know their expected sickness, s, which we normalize as expected spending in the generous plan. Sicker people will value the more generous policy over their healthier brethren, because they will take greater advantage of its additional generosity. This differential value is represented as $V(s)$, where V increases with s.

Suppose that the employee charge to enroll in the more generous plan is D, for differential. All individuals who have $V(s) > D$ will enroll in the more generous plan; those who have $V(s) < D$ will choose the moderate plan. We denote enrollment in the moderate plan as a function $s^*(D)$. As D increases, so does s^*.

We now need to consider plan premiums and the employer's pricing decision. In general, we would expect the moderate plan to cost less than the generous plan for anyone. Moreover, the sicker the individual, the greater will be the differential in resource costs between the plans. We denote the cost for a person enrolled in the moderate plan as αs, where $\alpha < 1$. Miller and Luft (1994), for example, estimate, in comparing HMOs with fee-for-service plans, that $\alpha = .9$.

Denote the mean level of s for $s > s^*$ as s_G, with s_M the mean for $s < s^*$, where the subscripts denote "generous" and "moderate." These means are the spending per person enrolled respectively in the generous and moderate plans. If plans offer policies with no administrative load, then $P_G = s_G$ and $P_M = \alpha s_M$ where P denotes the plan premium. The premium difference between the plans is

$$P_G - P_M = s_G - \alpha s_M = (1 - \alpha)\, s_M + (s_G - s_M). \tag{1.1}$$

The premium difference depends on two factors. The first is the resource cost savings in the less generous plan, $(1 - \alpha)s_M$. The second factor is adverse selection; sicker people are more likely to be enrolled in the more generous plan $(s_G - s_M)$.

Not all of the difference in plan premiums need be translated into differences in employee costs. Employers may make employees pay none, some, or all of the additional cost of the more generous policy. We consider two cases: In the equal-contribution case, the employer pays a fixed dollar subsidy independent of plan, and the employee pays the difference between the subsidy and the premium for his plan. In the proportional-subsidy case, the employer pays a fixed proportion of the premium cost of whatever plan the employee chooses, and the employee pays the rest. Holding plan design fixed, the interplay between the employer's pricing rules and the distribution of sickness in the population determines the severity of adverse selection.

Figure 1.2 shows a possible situation with the equal-contribution approach. Sickness, s, is assumed to be distributed uniformly from 0 to 1. The $V(s)$ curve is upward sloping, reflecting the increased value of the more generous plan as s increases. The curve labeled "Actual difference" shows the difference between the two plans in costs of medical care for a person of sickness s. Efficiency is achieved where the cost for the individual equals the gain in value he receives from the plan, as shown at point A. Efficiency requires that everyone to the right of s_A be in the generous plan, and everyone to the left in the moderate plan.

However, the differential charges paid by employees reflect not their own incremental costs, but rather the difference in average costs between the two plans for people who have currently chosen them. The curve labeled "Employee charge (equal contribution)" reflects the difference in what employees would pay as a function of s^*, assuming s^* were the dividing line for plan choice: That is, those with sickness above s^* choose the generous plan and those with sickness below s^* choose the moderate plan (we assume that $\alpha = .9$). Given equal contributions by the employer, equilibrium in the market is achieved where the charged difference equals $V(s)$; at point E_C.

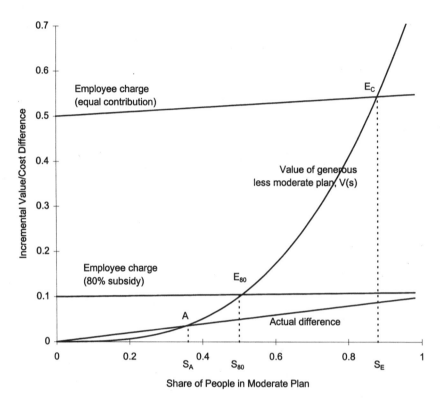

Figure 1.2
Plan choice equilibria

The actual equilibrium is far from efficient—many fewer people will be in the generous plan than ought to be in that plan. Indeed, for some combinations of $V(s)$, α, and the distribution of s, the generous plan empties completely. This is termed an "adverse selection death spiral."

Initially, the fact that the equal-contribution rule is inefficient may be surprising for economists, who believe that subsidies should be constant across alternatives. For example, if employers were giving employees choices among computers, an equal-contribution rule— "Here's a fixed subsidy, pick the computer you want"—would be optimal. However, the cost of a health plan depends on who chooses it. The same is not true for computers; hence, the equal-contribution rule is efficient in the computer example because the individual pays the difference in cost if he chooses a better computer. The equal-contribution approach to health plans fails because it does not charge individuals the difference in costs that they impose when choosing one plan over another. Rather, it charges individuals the difference in average costs for people who choose the different plans, and populations can vary dramatically from plan to plan because of adverse selection.

For health insurance plans, the optimal second-best single charge is roughly the average difference for all individuals who have little or no preference between the two plans. The cost difference for the marginal individual, not the average individual, is the appropriate basis for pricing those who currently have to decide among plans.

A common alternative approach for employer subsidies is to pay a constant percentage of the premium, implying that some plans get a greater dollar subsidy than others. Figure 1.2 shows a proportional plan with an 80% subsidy. The equilibrium is at E_{80}. Note that far fewer individuals choose the moderate plans with the proportional-subsidy than with the equal-contribution rule. Within a fixed employer budget, the proportional subsidy has the employer pay more and the employee less for the generous plan. Hence, it gets chosen more often. In effect, proportional subsidies provide an indirect approach to "risk adjusting" plan payments, a topic we return to below.

At the outset, we mentioned three difficulties arising from adverse selection. We now briefly discuss the other two.

Loss of Risk Spreading   The second loss from adverse selection results from less than optimal risk spreading. In the adverse-selection equilibrium, sick people pay substantially more for health insurance than healthy people because they choose the more expensive plan and because they are mixed in with other sick people. If we asked people in advance, they would want to insure against the risk that they will be high cost and thus would prefer the generous and more expensive policy. They would want to insure still more if there were additional costs due to adverse selection. Yet there is no way to purchase insurance against the condition of wanting high coverage; the absence of a market generates an efficiency loss.

Consider three polar pricing approaches for two plans: (1) charging the employee the same amount for each plan; (2) charging employees the actual difference in their expected costs across plans; and (3) making equal contributions across plans so that employees are charged the full difference in plan premiums. The first approach would spread risks fully but would suffer moral hazard: All insureds would pick the generous plan because it is available at no extra charge. The second approach would eliminate adverse selection, but there would still be a risk-spreading loss: The sick would spend more than the healthy for medical insurance. The third approach would have more risk-spreading losses than the second: Cost differences due to adverse selection would be added to actual cost differences.

If insureds could contract before knowing their condition, they would prefer a price difference lying between the first and second approaches, where the reduction in losses from moral hazard because the generous policy is insufficiently priced just balances the increased risk-spreading loss from increased premium differences. The policies would be priced closer together than their actuarially fair amounts and much closer together than the equal-contribution rule would produce.

Plan Manipulation   The third inefficiency from adverse selection derives from insurers' manipulation of plan offerings. The premiums that insurers are paid may not fully reflect their population mix, say because premiums are set in advance or because employers do not fully assess the mix of enrollees before bargaining with a plan over the premium. In such circumstances, premiums stay the same even if healthier people enter a plan or sick people leave it.

In such circumstances, insurers have incentives to attract healthy insureds and repel sick insureds, a process called risk selection. Employers usually prohibit insurers from merely denying enrollment to sick or high-cost people; insurers thus need more subtle methods. Utilization management—onerous processes for referrals or follow-up visits, or high copayments—disproportionately discourages high-intensity users. Discounts for memberships in health clubs might attract the right people, an outstanding oncology program the wrong ones.

Plans are also sensitive about what they are known to offer. The Massachusetts Group Insurance Commission (discussed below) conducted an informal study in 1994 of the mental health services of ten HMOs they offered their enrollees. Each claimed to enrollees to offer the minimum mental health coverage the state mandated. In fact, however, eight plans actually offered more generous benefits for critical cases. They did not advertise this fact because they wanted to avoid being selected against.[2]

---

2. Charles Slavin, personal communication, May 21, 1997.

Plan manipulation may impose significant losses, denying to both sick and healthy individuals the coverage they would most like. Even though people might pay a lot for the best cancer care, no plan may provide it.

II. A Tale of Two Entities

To examine adverse selection's empirical importance, we focus on the experience of two entities that allow individual choice among health insurance plans: Harvard University and the Group Insurance Commission (GIC) of Massachusetts (the purchasing group for state and local employees in Massachusetts). The two groups are similar in many respects: both offered a costly, generous plan and several HMOs (many of which serve both Harvard and the GIC); both have a long-term commitment to providing high-quality insurance; and both have been attempting to save money by reducing their health insurance costs over time. But the recent experiences of these two entities have been remarkably different, primarily because of how they have chosen to subsidize different health plans.

Harvard University

Harvard University offers health insurance to about 10,000 full- and part-time employees.[3] Beginning in 1992, Harvard offered two types of health plans: a generous PPO run by Blue Cross/Blue Shield of Massachusetts, and several HMOs. Figure 1.3 shows the real (1996$) premiums for a family policy in the PPO and the average HMO. (Throughout this chapter, all dollar amounts are in real (1996) dollars, and premiums and charges are for a family policy.[4]) In its first year, 1992, the PPO cost about $500 more than the HMOs, because in the absence of information about the enrollment mix, the initial price was set very high. Over the next two years, the PPO and HMO premiums converged to within $100 of each other.

---

3. See Cutler and Reber 1998 for more detail on the Harvard experience. For additional discussion of plan choice issues, see Feldman and Dowd (1993), Royalty and Solomon (1995), and Buchmueller and Feldstein (1996).
4. Some analyses use a weighted average of family and individual premiums. We choose instead to rely on a particular commodity found in the market.

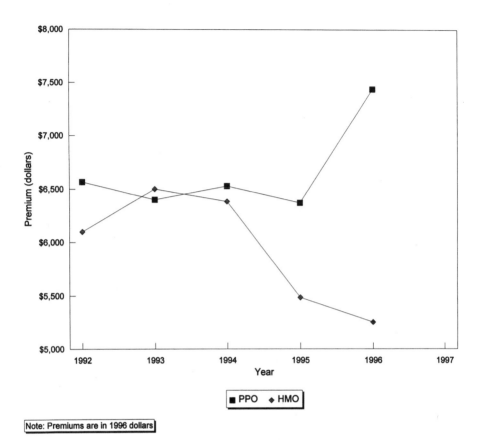

Figure 1.3
Real family premiums at Harvard

Because the premiums for the different plans were so similar, the PPO's additional cost to the employee was generally low. As figure 1.4 shows, between 1992 and 1994 employees paid an average of between $400 and $500 to enroll in the PPO instead of an HMO.[5] The figure also shows that enrollment in the PPO was stable at about 20% of Harvard employees.

In the mid-1990s, the University identified the rising cost of health benefits as an important culprit in the deficit it was facing. Harvard undertook a two-pronged response to the health cost increase. First, it

---

5. We ignore issues concerning these payments' tax status. Employee charges at Harvard are made on a pretax basis, so the after-tax contribution, in terms of consumption given up to enroll in the PPO, is smaller.

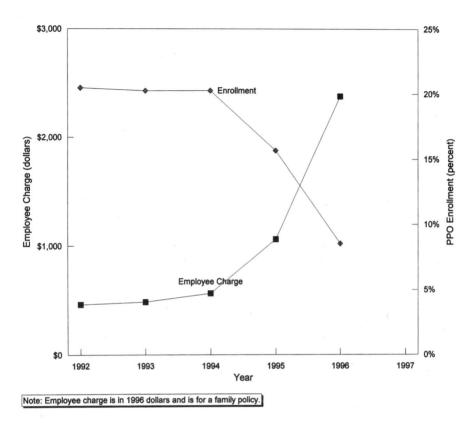

Note: Employee charge is in 1996 dollars and is for a family policy.

Figure 1.4
Real employee charge for the PPO and enrollment in the PPO at Harvard

implemented an equal-contribution rule for each of the plans. This arrangement began with about half of the employees in 1995; the other half joined in 1996.[6] Employees now pay the additional cost of more expensive plans. Second, Harvard engaged in strenuous negotiations with its health insurers, stressing that its new equal-contribution policy would produce large enrollment swings toward plans with lower rates and pressing its insurers to reduce their premiums.

HMO premiums fell substantially in 1995 in response to these measures—by close to $1,000 in real terms, as shown in figure 1.3. PPO premiums, in contrast, remained constant. This translated into a notable increase in the employee charges to enroll in the PPO, as shown in

---

6. Union contracts prohibited an immediate change for all unionized employees.

figure 1.4. In 1995, the cost of the PPO rose about $500, to roughly $1,000.

As expected, PPO enrollment fell as an initial response to this price increase. As figure 1.4 shows, PPO enrollment in 1995 fell from 20% to 15%, a significant response given that the change affected only half the employees that year. The employees who disenrolled from the PPO were healthier and younger than those who stayed (a mean age of 46 versus 51 years). As a result of the departure of healthy enrollees, the PPO lost money in 1995 and had to raise premiums in 1996.

The rise in premiums in 1996, combined with the change in policy for the remainder of the Harvard employees, resulted in a substantial increase in employee charges for the remaining PPO enrollees. As figure 1.4 shows, the required contribution for the PPO, which was about $500 in 1994, rose to more than $2,000 in 1996. Not surprisingly, enrollment in the PPO plummeted to about 9% of total employees. Those who left the plan were again younger than those who remained; the average age difference was five years. Blue Cross/Blue Shield's analysis showed that those who left the policy that year were 20% healthier than the average employee in the year before they left. As a result, the PPO lost substantial money once again. By the beginning of the 1997 rate negotiation period, it was clear that the PPO premium and charges would have to increase dramatically for the plan to break even. This was untenable both to the University and Blue Cross/Blue Shield, and the PPO was disbanded. Harvard's health insurance system lost its heavily populated PPO within three years of moving to an equal-contribution arrangement. The adverse selection death spiral twisted swiftly.

The Group Insurance Commission

The GIC provides insurance to roughly 133,000 employees and 245,000 total lives, making it one of the largest insurance purchasers in New England and many times larger than Harvard. As the 1990s began, the GIC, like Harvard, offered a traditional, more generous and costly indemnity policy and a passel of HMOs.

Figure 1.5 shows premiums the insurance plans charged the GIC. The annual premium for the indemnity policy was roughly $2,500 higher than the HMOs' premiums. Employees paid 10% of the cost for the policy in which they enrolled and the state paid the remaining 90%;

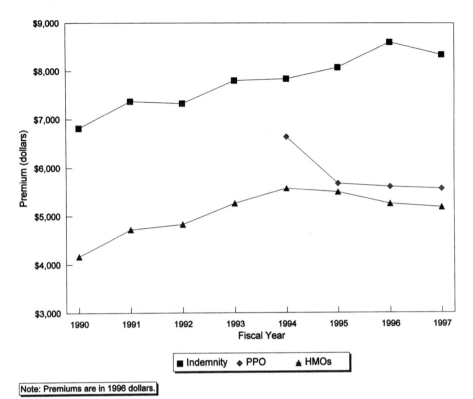

Figure 1.5
Real family premiums in the GIC

in 1995 the employee share was increased to 15%.[7] The legislature sets these employee shares. (Most legislators are believed to be enrolled in the generous indemnity policy.) Such proportional subsidies heavily subsidize the high-cost policies. As figure 1.6 shows, the indemnity policy cost employees only about $600 more than an HMO. Enrollment in the indemnity policy was relatively constant from 1990 to 1994 at about 30% (see figure 1.7).

In 1994, the GIC consolidated a number of Blue Cross/Blue Shield HMOs into a PPO, also offered by Blue Cross/Blue Shield. The plan change was intended partly to eliminate some marginally performing

---

7. Most employees accepted a small add-on to the indemnity policy for a catastrophic rider that increased the employee charge for the indemnity plan to about 15% through 1994 and about 20% after 1995.

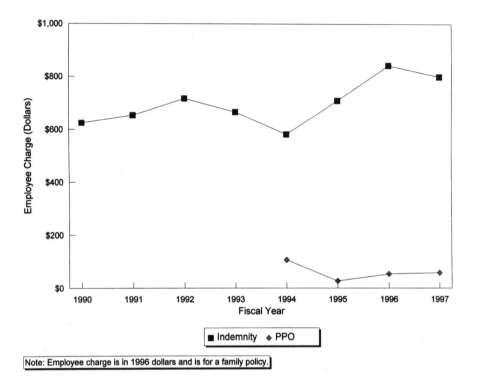

Figure 1.6
Real employee charge for indemnity and PPO policies at the GIC

HMOs and partly to encourage relatively healthy HMO enrollees to move into the experience-rated PPO and indemnity plan. This effort largely succeeded; the PPO drew a number of people from the HMOs, and enrollment in the indemnity policy actually increased. The risk mix in the PPO was sufficiently favorable that in 1995 the PPO premium fell to a level roughly equal to that of the HMOs.

The GIC thus appears to offer a quite stable plan menu. But over the course of the 1990s, adverse selection has been a serious issue. The indemnity policy has slowly been losing population, dropping to 27% of all enrollees by 1997. Real premiums for the HMOs have been flat or falling in recent years, whereas the costs of the indemnity policy have continued to rise. Real HMO premiums declined $400 between 1994 and 1997; real premiums for the indemnity policy rose over $500 (see figure 1.5). The reduction in HMO premium growth is not unique to the GIC: HMO premiums have not increased substantially in the Boston area for the past few years (Cutler and Reber 1998).

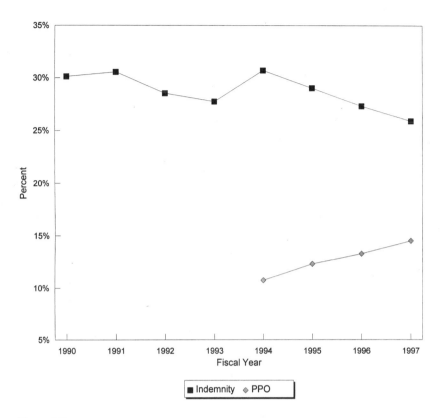

Figure 1.7
Enrollment in indemnity and PPO policies at the GIC

To examine the importance of adverse selection in the GIC's health insurance plans, and to consider potential solutions to the adverse-selection problem, we obtained detailed data on all the health insurance claims of GIC enrollees over the 30-month period encompassing fiscal years 1994 and 1995 and the first half of fiscal year 1996. With 245,000 total lives covered, the number of claims is quite large: nearly 65,000 hospital admissions and almost 15 million outpatient records.

The distribution of medical spending in the GIC pool is heavily skewed, as it is nationally. The upper 10% of people in a year (that is, the 10% with the highest medical expenditures) account for two-thirds of the total dollars spent; indeed, the top 1% of spenders account for nearly 30% of medical dollars (see table 1.1). This is very close to the distribution of spending found in national samples (Berk and Monheit 1992). Table 1.2 shows the share of enrollees in each type of plan in

Table 1.1
Distribution of spending in the GIC

Percentile	Amount	Cumulative share
Mean	$1,944	—
10th	$60	0.2%
25th	174	1.0
50th	507	5.1
75th	1,433	16.4
90th	3,955	34.4
99th	24,414	72.8

Note: The data are for individuals in fiscal year 1994. There are 180,837 observations.

Table 1.2
Age distribution across insurance plans, GIC data

| Measure | Plan | | |
	Indemnity	PPO	HMOs
Number of enrollees	76,185	22,434	128,709
Percent of enrollees, by age			
<1	0%	1%	0%
1–19	14	23	23
20–44	36	50	50
45–64	42	24	23
65+	8	1	4
Total	100%	100%	100%
Spending index	$1,623	$1,194	$1,264
[Ratio to HMO]	[1.28]	[0.94]	[1.00]

Note: Data are for fiscal year 1994. The spending index is an average of the age and sex distribution of enrollees weighted by average spending in 1987.

1994 by age.[8] The HMOs had 27% of their enrollees above age 45 and the PPO had 25%, whereas the indemnity plan had 50% above 45. Because medical spending is substantially greater for the old than for the young, these mix differentials have significant implications for cost.

The last two rows of table 1.2 provide summary measures for demographic selection. Using data from the 1987 National Medical Expenditure Survey, we computed average spending by age[9] and gender. We then formed a weighted average of "projected spending" in each plan using the plan's demographic enrollment shares as weights. The average HMO enrollee was predicted to spend $1,264; in contrast, predicted spending in the indemnity policy was 28% higher ($1,623). Recall that the premium for the indemnity policy is about 40% higher than the premium for the HMOs; the demographic mix of enrollees explains 28/40, or more two-thirds, of that difference.

Selection by age tells only a part of the story. For example, people of a given age who do not expect to need substantial medical care are likely to opt out of the indemnity plan, whereas those who do will opt in. To examine the importance of selection by health status, we focused on two important conditions for the under-65 population: pregnancy and heart attacks. Both are expensive; births cost several thousand dollars on average and heart attack costs average nearly $25,000.

Table 1.3 shows age- and gender-adjusted incidence rates for pregnancy and heart attacks. In each case, we found the rates in each plan by five-year age group (women aged 15–44 for pregnancy, men and women aged 45–64 for heart attacks) and then calculated a weighted average for each type of plan.[10] Both pregnancy and heart attack rates are higher in the indemnity plans than in the PPO, and both are higher in the PPO than in the HMOs. The differences are fairly large: After adjusting for age and sex, individuals in the indemnity plan have 30% more pregnancies and 90% more heart attacks than those in the HMOs.

We used claims information on individuals in the first two years of enrollment, 1994 and 1995, to examine whether selection is increasing

---

8. The GIC reimburses plans the same amount for each enrollee regardless of age and requires plans to accept anyone who wants to enroll in the plan. Hence, differential selection by age is an important form of adverse selection.

9. We divided the population into nine groups: <1, 1–4, 5–14, 15–24, 25–34, 35–44, 45–54, 55–64, and 65+.

10. The weights are the share of the GIC's entire population in that age and gender group.

Table 1.3
Age- and gender-adjusted incidence of plan utilization, GIC data

	Percent with condition, by plan		
Condition	Indemnity	PPO	HMOs
Pregnancy	3.4%	2.8%	2.5%
Heart attack	0.51%	0.34%	0.27%

Note: Pregnancy rate is for women aged 15–44. Heart attack rate is for those aged 45–64. Both rates are standardized to the age and gender distribution for the group as a whole using five-year age and gender (for heart attack) groups.

or falling over time. Overall, transitions among plans are relatively small. About 2% of people move from the indemnity plan to an HMO each year, and about 1% move in the reverse direction. The stickiness of plan choice from year to year is consistent with the evidence in Neipp and Zeckhauser 1985. Of course, the proportion of switchers might increase, as Harvard saw, if the indemnity plan were to lose its "excess" subsidy, so that the charge for the indemnity plan would jump substantially.

Table 1.4 summarizes individuals' medical spending before and after they switch plans. We show the share of switchers by their quartile in the spending distribution before they switched (1994) and again after they switched (1995). If movement between plans were random, the percentage in each cell would be 25%. The table's first column shows that 43% of the people who moved from the indemnity plan to an HMO were in the lowest quartile of spenders in the indemnity plan in 1994. By contrast, the third and fourth quartiles of spending were underrepresented among movers. In the subsequent year, people who moved to an HMO spent slightly less than average, with 53% being below median.

Among movers from HMOs to the indemnity policy, the shares are about 25% in each cell. Thus, those leaving the HMOs are not those who are particularly expensive to treat in either an HMO or in an indemnity setting.

These patterns of movement tell an intriguing story of adverse selection, somewhat at variance with the traditional account within economics. In recent GIC experience, at least, adverse selection occurs because low-risk people drop out of generous, high-cost plans; the selection into high-cost plans of high-risk people is not a significant factor. Since costs are skewed on the high end, not the low, such dynamics affect the mix of costs less quickly.

Table 1.4
Transition of families by plan and position in spending distribution, GIC data

Spending quartile	Indemnity → HMO (1.8% of indemnity enrollees)		HMO → Indemnity (0.9% of HMO enrollees)	
	Indemnity	HMO	HMO	Indemnity
1st (lowest)	43%	29%	26%	26%
2nd	26	24	22	19
3rd	15	27	25	27
4th (highest)	16	21	27	29
Total	100%	100%	100%	100%
Average Spending				
All	$6,833	$3,668	$3,173	$6,941
Movers	4,646	4,445	4,865	7,987
Ratio	68%	121%	153%	115%

Note: Transitions to or from the PPO are not included.

The GIC commissioners have noted that the GIC plans are increasingly subject to adverse selection. Over the past several years, the GIC has taken several steps to enhance the indemnity policy's viability. First, it has made sure that budget savings apply to all plans roughly equally. For example, when the state needed to save money in 1992, cost sharing was increased for both HMOs and the indemnity plan, leaving the relative generosity of the plans roughly unchanged, even though some commissioners thought the indemnity plan should have been reduced more.[11]

Perhaps most important, however, the GIC has been actively involved in managing the indemnity plan to reduce its costs. In 1992, for example, the GIC completed a "carve out" of pharmacy benefits in the indemnity plan, subsequently extended to the PPO when it was established in 1994. Most pharmacy benefits are now provided on a mail-order basis, with a pharmacy PPO providing the rest. Bulk purchasing allows the GIC to save money on prescription drugs. Similarly, in 1994 the GIC "carved out" mental health and substance abuse benefits from

---

11. Indeed, the GIC commissioned a relative-value analysis of its 1996 plans (Group Insurance Commission 1995). The difference between the most and least generous plans was just 1.3%. By contrast, the indemnity plan had a premium 90% above the cheapest plan and 40% above the second most expensive plan. The relative value calculation looked solely at plan benefits and did not take into account how vigorously a plan was managed. Had it done so, it would have weakened the HMOs' relative values.

the indemnity and PPO plans. When a person in either of these plans needs mental health services, these services are managed by a company that specializes in these conditions. As a result of the carve out, mental health expenditures have fallen from $25 million to $10 million per year (in nominal terms). The indemnity plan also manages outpatient benefits more tightly than a traditional indemnity policy does. High-cost outpatient users are now identified and their care is reviewed for appropriateness. And the indemnity plan has an exclusive contract with an outpatient laboratory service for nonemergency services; again, bulk purchasing brings price discounts. Finally, using the leverage of substitution on laboratory services, the indemnity plan has bargained with its twenty-five highest cost hospitals in Massachusetts for lower rates.

As a final measure, the GIC is undertaking a thorough study of the health status of the individuals in its different plans and their care utilization. From the results of this study, the GIC may undertake a risk adjustment scheme for its health insurance plans. Appropriate risk adjustment in pricing has the potential to diminish substantially any problems from adverse selection, as we discuss in the next section.

Summary

Our case studies suggest that adverse selection is a significant factor among employer-based health plans. In both the entities we examine, adverse selection became an important issue in recent years. And in both cases, the proximate reason for adverse selection is the same: healthy people selected out of the most generous plan as the cost of the less generous policies fell. At Harvard, the problem was not fully recognized until after the effects were known; at the GIC, the problem has been recognized, but no long-term solution has yet been implemented.

III. Strategies to Deter Adverse Selection

The most immediate issue raised by the experiences of Harvard and the GIC is, If an employer wants to deter adverse selection across insurance plans, how should it do so? How can we encourage individuals to select appropriate plans—plans they would choose if they faced the true costs they would impose by choosing one plan over another?

One possibility would be to look at individuals' characteristics, then assign them to appropriate plans, given geographic location, health status, and announced preferences. But such an approach would run contrary to the norms of our nation and the movements of the health sector in recent years toward greater choice for consumers and greater competition among health plans. We therefore confine our analysis to decentralized systems, in which individuals choose from a menu with varied plans and contribution rates.

Can we have such freedom of choice but avoid severe problems of adverse selection? Standardizing plans (e.g., requiring the same coverage in all plans) might help. That way, those with particular concerns, say mental health visits or diabetes care, would not migrate among plans to the one most generous for their needs. Indeed, the GIC staff recently proposed standardizing a variety of aspects of insurance plans, with adverse selection concerns in mind.[12] Debate on standardization frequently focuses on the particulars of the benefits to be standardized.[13]

There is another issue as well. Standardizing plan offerings may impede valuable competition on program design. For example, if the employer standardizes drug copayments (say for formulary generic, formulary brand name, and nonformulary brand name), HMOs will be inhibited in designing better plans on this dimension. And what is right for one plan may not be right for other plans, depending on the ability of plans to manage utilization or negotiate with providers. HMOs might not want limits on the number of well-baby care visits, for example, preferring to let people have all the visits their providers can spare, while fee-for-service plans may find such limits valuable. The greater the employer's confidence that he knows the optimal design of coverage and that this is optimal across plans, the more willing he should be to standardize plan choices. But standardization is not always called for.

---

12. The proposal was for all plans to remove the $1 million cap on lifetime expenditures; mandate a minimum of 80% coverage on durable medical equipment and appliances; mandate out-of-network benefits for mental health; set a $1,000 maximum benefit for hearing aids; set standard visits and copayments for occupational, speech, and physical therapy; allow annual pediatric exams up to age eighteen; implement a uniform $10 copayment for formulary drugs and $15 copayment for brand name nonformulary drugs; and standardize vaccination and immunization coverage.
13. One of the authors of this chapter, for example, speculates that the copay charges for different types of drugs were likely set too close together.

Even if plans are standardized, however, they will still have disparate populations. If we wish to know the true cost of plans, the prices to charge employees if they are to make efficient choices, we will have to adjust for these disparities in plan enrollment. The employer can still offer freedom of choice, if he can price appropriately. Appropriate pricing means charging less than a plan costs if it has disproportionate numbers of high-risk people, and more than a plan costs if it disproportionately enrolls healthier people. In essence, we must adjust prices to account for the risk mix in each plan. This section evaluates four potential mechanisms for risk adjustment.

Premium Subsidies

The crudest, albeit best-known, method of risk adjustment is the one that Harvard employed prior to 1995 and that the GIC still employs: subsidize the premium of the most generous policy so that it is more affordable than risk differences alone would indicate. Although this solution has historically been the most common way to deter adverse selection, we do not believe it is the most appropriate solution. To begin with, it pays no attention to the actual composition of populations within health plans; it simply assumes that if a plan is more expensive, this must be due to a worse mix of enrollees. Although subsidizing premiums deters adverse selection, it also reduces the incentives for employees to choose their health insurance plans efficiently. Moreover, it eliminates many incentives for plans to operate efficiently or price competitively. Suppose, for example, that the most expensive plan raises its premium by $1 in an effort to boost profits. If the employer is subsidizing the expensive policy by 90%, employees will see only a $.10 increase in price. This substantially limits employees' incentives to seek out the most cost-effective plans.

A comparison of Harvard University and the GIC (Hill and Wolfe (1997) also discuss this issue) provides some tentative evidence on the effect of subsidy rates on premiums. As table 1.5 shows, real HMO premiums fell more rapidly at Harvard after it implemented the equal-contribution rule (9.7% annually between 1994 and 1996) than they did at the GIC (2.9% annually) in the same period. Indeed, figure 1.3 shows a large decline in premiums at Harvard in 1995, the year the equal-contribution rule was implemented. This premium reduction was not matched at the GIC, despite the similarities of the policies offered. The more rapid decline in HMO premiums at Harvard did not merely

Table 1.5
Change in Real HMO Premiums, Harvard and the GIC

Period	Annual percentage change	
	Harvard	GIC
1990–94	4.9%	7.3%
1994–96	–9.7%	–2.9%

Note: Each entry is the average annual percentage change in real family premiums. Premiums are weighted across HMOs using contemporaneous enrollment rates.

offset more rapid premium growth prior to 1994; between 1990 and 1994, real premium growth at Harvard was also below the level at the GIC. This suggests that the equal-contribution rule resulted in premium reductions for Harvard employees in HMOs.

We suspect that marginal subsidies to more expensive plans result in higher charges from the plans than would have otherwise prevailed. Because one goal for employers is to realize the lowest premiums possible, perpetuating a marginal subsidy to high-cost plans does not seem like the appropriate solution.

Reinsurance

The highest-cost users account for a large share of medical expenditures. Thus, having mandatory reinsurance for high-cost people could be one way to risk adjust premiums.[14] Suppose that all expenses over a certain amount (perhaps $25,000 annually) were paid for out of a central account funded by a uniform tax on all insurance premiums. Then, plans would pay for high-cost users in proportion to total revenues in their plan, not the specific enrollment of the high-cost group. If the high-cost group were primarily responsible for the high costs of the more generous plans, this could reduce the adverse selection problem. The compensating danger is that once the expenses of high-cost users are pooled, the plans lose the incentive to monitor their utilization.

The reinsurance strategy parallels the mental health/substance abuse carve out. In that case, all spending for a particular condition is removed from plan premiums; in the reinsurance case, all spending above a certain amount is removed from plan premiums. The implicit

---

14. See Cutler and Zeckhauser 1997 for a more general discussion of reinsurance.

rationale is that the individuals carved out, whether by condition or expense level, account for most of the adverse selection, measured on a dollar basis.

How much of the difference in costs would reinsurance overcome? If high spenders are the problem, then reinsurance may be the solution. Figure 1.8 shows the share of the difference between the indemnity policy and the HMOs at the GIC accounted for by particular parts of the spending distribution. For example, the last bar in the figure shows that spending in amounts above $100,000 per person accounts for only 5% of the total spending difference between the two sets of plans.[15] Indeed, spending above $25,000 per year accounts for only 8% of the difference in spending between more-generous and less-generous plans. Contrary to what many would expect, the vast bulk of the difference between the plans is that small users in the indemnity policy average much higher annual claims than in the HMO. Spending in amounts below $5,000 per person accounts for two-thirds of the overall differences in plan costs. This may result from more severe moral hazard in the indemnity policy, different prices paid for services, or less restrictive use of gatekeepers.

If risk mixes for patients who are not extremely expensive to treat differ substantially among plans, then reinsurance for high-cost users does not significantly reduce the consequences of adverse selection.

Prospective and Retrospective Risk Adjustment

The final two methods of risk adjustment are prospective and retro-spective adjustment. Older people, women of childbearing age, and people with certain conditions spend more on medical care than those in other groups or without those conditions. Thus, if we could measure the distribution of plan enrollees ex ante or ex post, we could adjust per capita payments to each plan to account for these differences. If the plans were compensated for the differences in risk among their in-sureds, then in a competitive market premiums would differ only by their pure efficiency differences.

Using the notation of Section II, suppose we observed s_G and s_M, the average healthiness of enrollees in the more- and less-generous poli-cies. We could then set employer payments across plans of $E_G = s_G$ and

---

15. Note that this is not total spending of people using over $100,000 of services in a year but rather the amount of that spending that is above $100,000. Under a reinsurance system, this is the amount that would be reinsured.

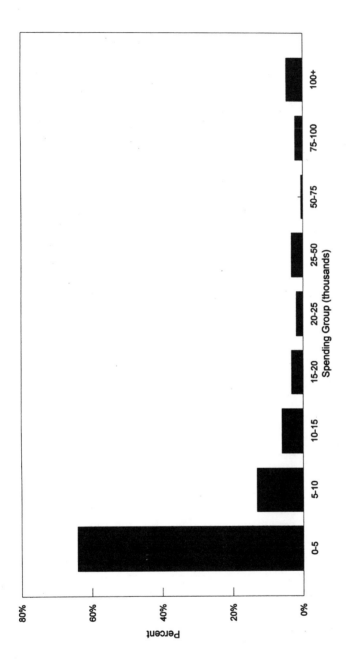

Figure 1.8
Share of total cost difference by spending level, GIC

$E_M = s_M$. Because these payments would eliminate the bias in employee charges caused by adverse selection, the only difference in charges facing employees would be the efficiency savings in the moderate plan. This charge arrangement would provide employees with appropriate incentives to choose the most efficient plan.[16]

Measuring risk differences ex ante is termed prospective risk adjustment; measuring risk differences ex post is termed retrospective risk adjustment. If these methods can be implemented effectively, they yield the right prices, and individual choices produce an efficient outcome. The major question is whether all the factors that influence costs can be observed. For example, not all people with high blood pressure have a major cardiovascular incident. If among those with high blood pressure, the people who sense they are more likely to have a major incident select into the more generous policy, a risk adjustment strategy based only on the presence or absence of high blood pressure would be incomplete.

The incompleteness of risk adjustment is problematic because the distribution of medical spending is so skewed. If individuals know they will be in the extreme tail of the spending distribution because of factors we cannot observe, adverse selection can still be economically important even if risk adjustment is good "on average." Our GIC data suggested that most of the difference in costs across plans was not in the distribution's tail. The experience of other entities may differ, perhaps because of differing historical patterns of plan offerings.

Prospective or retrospective risk adjustment is severely hindered if insurers can alter their coding practices in light of the risk adjustment system. For example, if employers pay a surcharge to plans that enroll people with high blood pressure and insurers pay particular attention to noting whether a person has that diagnosis, the risk adjustment system depends as much on insurers' ability and willingness to record this information accurately as on the true incidence in the population. Indeed, this "upcoding" problem was particularly severe with the implementation of the DRG rating system for Medicare (Carter and Ginsberg 1985).

Research on effective risk adjustment methods has been progressing rapidly (see Newhouse, Beeuwkes, and Chapman 1997 for a review).

---

16. This works well if health plan choice depends only on s, so that the cost savings for the marginal person, with no preference among the plans, appropriately guides the market. But if personal preferences also play a role (if, for example, some low s people particularly like the indemnity plan), the correct price would be different for each person, and charging everyone the same price would not be efficient.

Current methods of prospective risk adjustment can explain about 5–10% of the variance in individual medical spending. Although this percentage is not large, in designing a risk adjustment system we care about the share of expected medical spending that can be explained, not actual medical spending. Estimates of the difference between expected and actual medical spending suggest that expected spending differences are about 20–25% of actual spending differences, so that current risk adjustment systems achieve 20% (5/25) to 50% (10/20) of ideal effectiveness.

Whether this degree of success—with or without reinsurance—is enough to limit adverse selection, we do not know. To date, there have been few experiments involving insurance choice in a system with risk adjustment that would allow us to provide an answer.

IV. Conclusions

Most Americans receive health insurance through plans administered and subsidized by employers. Typically, charges to employees depend on the plan they choose—the higher the premium to the employer, the higher the charge to employees, with the result that people who choose more generous insurance policies must pay to subsidize the sicker people who choose the more expensive policy. This arrangement invites adverse selection.

The experiences of Harvard University, which provides equal contributions across plans, and the Massachusetts GIC, which subsidizes 85% of premiums regardless of plan cost, show that adverse selection is a real-world concern. Harvard's PPO crashed in a death spiral when Harvard implemented an equal-contribution rule. Adverse selection was so great that the most generous policy could not be offered at a reasonable price. The GIC has avoided such a situation, in part by not moving to an equal-contribution rule and in part by undertaking steps to reduce the most generous plan's costs. This has been challenging, however, and adverse selection remains a concern.

To motivate the right insureds to choose the right plans, employers who offer employees a choice among plans should charge them the additional cost the employee would incur in the more generous plan. The mixes of insureds in the actual plans should not affect charges to employees; only the cost savings for a particular individual should affect his decision. In such a system, employers vary the premium across plans based on ex ante differences in demographics and observed health status across plans and may make further corrections to payments based on ex post claims experience. Careful empirical assessment is essential to guide this process. For example, two of our most important findings about the GIC were surprises: Spending above $25,000 per year accounted for only 8% of the difference in costs between the indemnity and HMO policies, and the vast majority of adverse selection resulted from the movement of low-risk employees. Implementing a carefully designed and empirically informed risk adjustment system is essential to making health insurance competition work well.

References

Berk, Mark L., and Alan C. Monheit. 1992. "The Concentration of Medical Expenditures: An Update." *Health Affairs* 11(4): 145–49.

Buchmueller, Thomas C., and Paul J. Feldstein. 1996. "Consumers' Sensitivity to Health Plan Premiums: Evidence from a Natural Experiment in California." *Health Affairs* XV (Spring): 143–151.

Carter, Grace, and Paul B. Ginsberg. 1985. The Medicare Case Mix Index Increase: Medical Practice Changes, Aging, and DRG Creep. Rand R-3292.

Cutler, David M. 1996. "Restructuring Medicare for the Future." In *Setting National Priorities*, ed. Robert Reischauer. Washington, DC: The Brookings Institution, 197–233.

Cutler, David M., and Sarah Reber. 1998. "Paying for Health Insurance: The Tradeoff Between Competition and Adverse Selection." forthcoming *Quarterly Journal of Economics*, May.

Cutler, David M., and Richard J. Zeckhauser. 1997. "Reinsurance for Catastrophes and Cataclysms." Working Paper no. 5913, National Bureau of Economic Research, Cambridge, MA.

Feldman, Roger, and Bryan Dowd. 1993. The Effectiveness of Managed Competition: Results from a Natural Experiment. Institute for Health Services Research, University of Minnesota.

Group Insurance Commission. 1995. "Relative Value Analysis of GIC Plans." Boston, MA: Group Insurance Commission.

Hill, Stephen C., and Barbara Wolfe. 1997. "Testing the HMO Competitive Strategy: An Analysis of Its Impact on Medical Care Resources," *Journal of Health Economics* 16(3), 261–286.

Miller, Robert, and Harold Luft. 1994. "Managed Care Plan Performance Since 1980." *Journal of the American Medical Association* (May 18): 1512–9.

Neipp, Joachim, and Richard Zeckhauser. 1985. "Persistence in the Choice of Health Plans." In *Advances in Health Economics and Health Services Research*, vol. 6, ed. R. M. Scheffler and L. F. Rossiter, 47–74. Greenwich, CT: JAI Press.

Newhouse, Joseph P., Melinda Beeuwkes, and John D. Chapman. 1997. "Risk Adjustment and Medicare." Harvard University. Mimeographed.

Rothschild, Michael, and Joseph E. Stiglitz. 1976. "Equilibrium in Competitive Insurance Markets: An Essay on the Economics of Imperfect Information." *Quarterly Journal of Economics* 80:629–49.

Royalty, Anne Beeson, and Neil Soloman. 1995. "Health Plan Choice: Price Elasticities in a Managed Competition Setting." Mimeo, Stanford University, October 1995.

2

Is Price Inflation Different for the Elderly?
An Empirical Analysis of Prescription Drugs

Ernst R. Berndt, *MIT Sloan School of Management and NBER*
Iain M. Cockburn, *University of British Columbia and NBER*
Douglas L. Cocks, *Eli Lilly and Company*
Arnold M. Epstein, M.D., *Harvard Medical School*
Zvi Griliches, *Harvard University and NBER*

Executive Summary

Recently controversy has surrounded the issue of whether Social Security payments to the elderly should continue to be adjusted automatically according to changes in the Consumer Price Index (CPI). One issue in the public policy debate concerns whether price inflation is different for the elderly, particularly because the official Bureau of Labor Statistics price indexes for medical care have been growing more rapidly than the overall CPI, and medical care expenditures constitute a larger proportion of the elderly's budget than of the young's.

Using annual IMS data from 1990 to 1996, we examine empirically whether elderly-nonelderly price inflation differentials exist for prescription pharmaceuticals. We assess prices for prescription drugs destined for ultimate use by the elderly versus the nonelderly at three points in the distribution chain: initial sales from manufacturers, intermediate purchases by retail pharmacies, and final sales from retail pharmacies to patients or payors. We find that at the initial point in the distribution chain, no differences in price inflation exist for the aggregate of drugs destined for use by the elderly versus those for the nonelderly. At the intermediate sell-in point to pharmacy distribution, we examine antibiotics (ABs), antidepressants (ADs), and calcium channel blockers (CCBs). For ABs, since 1992 price inflation has been somewhat greater for the elderly than for the young, reflecting in part the elderly's more intensive use of newer branded products having fewer side effects, adverse drug interactions and more convenient dosing—attributes of particular importance to

The authors gratefully acknowledge research support from the National Science Foundation, the Alfred P. Sloan Foundation, and Eli Lilly and Company, as well as the considerable data support by Susan Capps and Sheila Gross from the Plymouth Group at IMS International, Dennis Fixler at the U.S. Bureau of Labor Statistics, and Robert Dribbon, Rhea Mihalison, and Douglas Treger from Merck & Co., Inc. We thank Thomas Croghan, M.D., David Cutler, and Alan Garber, M.D., for comments. The opinions and conclusions expressed in this paper are those of the authors and do not necessarily reflect views or positions of any of the organizations with which the authors are affiliated or those of any of the research sponsors.

the elderly. For ADs, price inflation is considerably less for the elderly than for the young, due in large part to the elderly's greater use of older generic products. For CCBs, elderly-nonelderly differentials are negligible. None of these differentials adjust for variations in quality.

At the final retail sell-out point, we examine only ADs. We find that because retailers obtain larger gross margins on generic than on branded products, and because the elderly are disproportionately large users of generic ADs, the elderly-nonelderly price inflation differential benefiting the elderly at the intermediate point is reduced considerably at final sale.

I. Introduction

Over the next few decades, the U.S. population aged 65 and older will grow both in absolute numbers and as a share of the total population. As people age, they tend to have higher medical care expenses. Thus an increasingly elderly society can be expected to devote a greater amount of its expenditures to medical care. The implications of a graying society for future medical care expenditures depend of course on both the price and the quantity of future medical care for the elderly.

To the extent that they live on fixed incomes, the elderly are particularly vulnerable to price inflation. Moreover, medical care price increases are likely to affect the elderly differentially, because medical care is a larger share of their current budgets. Recently there has been substantial controversy concerning the continued automatic adjustment of Social Security payments to the elderly on the basis of changes in the Consumer Price Index (CPI). A panel of experts estimates that the CPI overstates true cost-of-living increases by about 1.1% per year (U.S. Senate Finance Committee 1996).

Relatively little is known about the extent to which price inflation of the basket of medical care goods and services used by the elderly differs from the price inflation of the set of medical care goods and services used by younger Americans. In this chapter, we focus on elderly-nonelderly price inflation differentials for one component of medical care, namely, prescription pharmaceuticals, from 1990 to 1996.[1]

The systems by which prescription pharmaceuticals are distributed and paid for in the United States are complex and rapidly changing.

---

1. For a discussion of patterns in total acute care health expenditures by patient age group from 1953 to 1987, see Cutler and Meara 1997.

We assess elderly-nonelderly price differentials at three different points in the distribution chain: (1) the initial point involving sales from manufacturers to wholesalers, retailers, and hospitals; (2) an intermediate point at which retail pharmacies acquire prescription drugs from wholesalers and manufacturers; and (3) a final point at which retail pharmacies dispense and sell prescription drugs to patients. With respect to payors, at the retail sell-out point in the distribution chain, we distinguish consumers' out-of-pocket expenditures for pharmaceuticals from those expenditures involving government funds (Medicaid and various public assistance programs) as well as from payments by private, third-party insurance sources (fee-for-service insurance plans and various forms of "medigap" and managed care).

One potential reason for elderly-nonelderly drug price inflation differentials is that the brand-generic proportions could vary by age. For treatment of acute conditions, the elderly may be more fragile, and thus prudent medical practice might suggest prescribing for them the newest generation of drugs having the fewest side effects and adverse drug interactions and the most convenient dosing. Under this hypothesis, for certain acute conditions, one might expect the elderly to use newer, branded drugs disproportionately. To the extent newer, branded drugs increase in price more rapidly than older, off-patent and generic drugs, the elderly's bundle of drugs would be expected to increase more rapidly than that of the young.

Although the same considerations would apply for treatment of chronic conditions, the surviving elderly are more likely to be using older drug products, for physicians are hesitant to change medications when a particular existing drug regimen is working well in treating a chronic condition. Because they have stickier usage patterns and have survived to old age, the elderly would therefore disproportionately use older drugs, which are more often available as generics, to treat their chronic conditions. Under this hypothesis, drug price inflation for the elderly's bundle would be less than that for the young. We examine both these hypotheses empirically, focusing on three therapeutic classes—antibiotics, antidepressants and calcium channel blockers.

We begin in the next section by providing background information on various trends and demographic aspects of the U.S. medical care marketplace and summarizing the literature dealing with age differentials in the rate of health care price inflation. In Sections III, IV, and V we focus on prices at initial, intermediate, and final links of the distribution chain, respectively. We document and then examine implications of the fact that the elderly and nonelderly have differential uses of drugs across various therapeutic classes, and varying brand-generic consumption patterns within therapeutic classes. We compute and report on separate elderly-nonelderly price indexes, using a fixed-weight Laspeyres index that mimics procedures currently employed by the U.S. Bureau of Labor Statistics (BLS), and also employ a changing-share Divisia price index recommended for use by the CPI commission. We also comment on the important role of differential brand-generic gross margins at retail pharmacies. In section VI we summarize our findings, offer caveats, and outline important issues for future research.

II. Background

Health Care Expenditures

We begin by reviewing recent changes in the components, sources, location, and methods of payment for health care items with a particular focus on pharmaceuticals. In 1995, prescription drugs accounted for 6.3% of the $878.8 billion in total personal health expenditures, nonprescription drugs constituted 3.2%, professional medical services 34.1%, hospital care 39.8%, nursing home care 8.9%, home health care 3.3%, and supplies and other, the remaining 4.4%.[2]

The sources of funds for personal health expenditures varied considerably. Whereas consumers' out-of-pocket expenditures accounted for 18.3% of expenditures for physician services, 3.3% of those for hospital care, and 42.4% of those for nursing home care, direct consumer expenditures (including copayments and deductibles) constituted 39.5% of total prescription drug spending, down from 48.3% in 1990; private third-party insurance covered 39.8% of total prescription drug spending in 1994, up from 34.5% in 1990.[3]

The locus of prescription pharmaceutical sales is also undergoing change. In 1996, for example, about 57% of the money spent on pharmaceuticals involved retail sales (chain pharmacies, independents, mass merchandisers, and food stores), down from 64% in 1990.

---

2. Statistics in this and the following paragraph are taken from Levit et al. 1996, Table 1 (p. 179), Table 5 (p. 185), Table 12 (p. 206), Table 13 (p. 207), and Table 14 (p. 208).
3. In 1995 (1990), the portion of total prescription drug spending from governmental sources was 20.7% (17.0%).

Whereas the dollar share for mail order increased from 5% to 9%, that for hospitals, clinics, and nursing homes remained relatively constant, 28% in 1990 and 29% in 1996, as did that for staff model health maintenance organizations (HMOs)—2% in both years.[4]

Within the retail sector, method of payment has changed dramatically over the last several years. As table 2.1 shows, since 1991 the share of new prescriptions paid for by cash has fallen sharply from 59% to 32%, whereas that paid for directly by third-party sources other than Medicaid has doubled, increasing from 28% to 57%. Third-party insurance has now become the predominant method of payment for prescription pharmaceuticals sold in retail outlets. The Medicaid share of dollars has varied less, from a high of about 15% in 1993 to about 11% in 1996. (Note that Medicare does not cover outpatient pharmaceutical expenses.) In terms of numbers of new prescriptions, the 1990–96 average annual growth rate (AAGR) for cash customers is –6.6% vs. 20.5% for third-party payors.

The above discussion on health expenditures does not distinguish by age group. Through its annual Consumer Expenditure Survey (CES), the BLS collects data on consumers' out-of-pocket expenditures (OOPs) for various budget items, including components of health care. The CES's unit of observation is the consumer unit ("household"), defined as "the person/group of persons in the household who is/are independent of all other persons in the household for payment of their major expenses" (U.S. Department of Commerce 1994, 3). The person in the consumer unit (CU) with major financial responsibility for payment of housing expenses is called the reference person ("head of household") of the consumer unit. CUs are stratified in a number of ways, including one of particular interest to us, namely, by age of the reference person. In tables 2.2 and 2.3 we summarize data from the 1990 and 1995 CES. Five points are particularly worth noting.

First, as one would expect, older Americans tend to have larger OOPs on medical care items and services than do the younger. The OOPs per CU health expenditure share generally grows with age, but it increases particularly sharply after age 65, as the top three panels of table 2.2 show. In 1995, for example, total OOP health-related expenditures for those under age 25 averaged $465, for those aged 55–64 it was $1,909, and for those 75 and over the average was $2,683. Whereas the average share of health care expenditures over all consumer units

---

4. IMS 1996 Class of Trade Analysis and Retail Method of Payment Analysis.

Table 2.1
Retail methods of payment, 1991–1996

Date	New prescriptions, in millions				New prescriptions, percentage distribution		
	Cash	MEDICAID	Third party	Total	Cash	MEDICAID	Third party
3Q91	262.4	59.3	122.2	443.9	59.1%	13.4%	27.5%
4Q91	279.2	66.8	136.3	482.3	57.9%	13.9%	28.3%
1Q92	268.6	67.5	140.9	477.0	56.3%	14.2%	29.5%
2Q92	262.5	65.3	140.9	468.7	56.0%	13.9%	30.1%
3Q92	254.0	65.8	137.1	456.9	55.6%	14.4%	30.0%
4Q92	268.2	72.0	151.9	492.1	54.5%	14.6%	30.9%
1Q93	259.1	74.4	165.2	498.7	52.0%	14.9%	33.1%
2Q93	247.0	71.1	164.8	482.9	51.1%	14.7%	34.2%
3Q93	233.5	69.5	164.0	467.0	50.0%	14.9%	35.1%
4Q93	250.1	76.3	186.4	512.8	48.8%	14.9%	36.3%
1Q94	232.4	69.5	201.4	503.3	46.2%	13.8%	40.0%
2Q94	225.2	67.5	205.9	498.6	45.2%	13.5%	41.3%
3Q94	215.5	63.4	205.4	484.3	44.5%	13.1%	42.4%
4Q94	222.2	66.7	229.0	517.9	42.9%	12.9%	44.2%
1Q95	213.9	70.6	251.7	536.2	39.9%	13.2%	46.9%
2Q95	200.5	66.1	252.0	518.6	38.7%	12.7%	48.6%
3Q95	192.7	63.9	251.9	508.5	37.9%	12.6%	49.5%
4Q95	199.8	68.2	282.2	550.2	36.3%	12.4%	51.3%
1Q96	192.8	67.6	291.8	552.2	34.9%	12.2%	52.8%
2Q96	180.0	61.5	294.2	535.7	33.6%	11.5%	54.9%
3Q96	176.6	60.3	296.3	533.2	33.1%	11.3%	55.5%
4Q96	183.6	65.7	325.5	574.8	31.9%	11.4%	56.6%
AAGR	−6.6%	2.0%	20.5%	5.0%			

Source: IMS America 1996.

in 1995 was 5.4%, for those under age 25 it was 2.5%, between ages 55 and 64 it was 5.9%, for those 65 and over it doubled to 11.9%, and for those 75 and over it increased further to 14.4%. Moreover, the data in table 2.2 reveal that the share of health care expenditures attributable to each age group was quite stable over 1990–95.[5]

Second, as the elderly constitute a greater proportion of the population, they account for an increasingly large and disproportionate percentage of the nation's total OOP health expenditures. As shown in the bottom three panels of table 2.2, whereas CUs over age 65 accounted for 20.7% of all consumer units in 1990, their larger per capita out-of-pocket health expenditures implied that the CUs over age 65 constituted 30.9% of OOP health expenditures over all age groups; by 1995, these numbers increased slightly to 21.1% and 32.3%, respectively.[6] Interestingly, the proportion of consumer units aged 65–74 decreased very slightly between 1990 and 1995, from 11.7% to 11.6%, but the percentage of consumer units aged 75 and over increased more sharply, from 9.0% to 9.6%, resulting in an increase in their OOP health expenditures share over all age groups from 13.5% to 14.8%.

Third, although total OOPs health care expenditure patterns may be stable, since 1990 people of all ages (and especially the elderly) appear to have significantly substituted payments to health insurance for direct payments for professional medical services, drugs, and medical supplies.[7] Note that in the CES, consumer OOP expenditures for health insurance are the sum of employees' pretax contributions at work and direct health insurance premium payments, but employers' health insurance contributions are not included, for those are treated as a business expense. As the second panel of table 2.3 shows, for all consumers the health insurance share increased from 39% to 50% between 1990 and 1995. For those under age 65, the 1995 health insurance share was about 45%, up from slightly under 40% in 1990; for the elderly, however, the increase was even greater, from 45% in 1990 to 58% in 1995. Thus by 1995 more than half of the elderly's OOPs health care budget was devoted to health insurance.

---

5. For comparisons back to 1980, see Acs and Sabelhaus 1995.
6. Note that these OOPs exclude all government funding, such as that for Medicare. Thus the 32% figure likely understates the elderly's proportion of total OOPs plus government health care expenditures.
7. Employers may also be shifting health insurance premium costs and copayments/deductibles to their employees. For discussion, see Baker and Kramer 1991 and Cowan et al. 1996.

Table 2.2
Out-of-pocket health care expenditures by reference person age group, United States, 1990 and 1995

Category	All consumers	Under 25	25–34	35–44	45–54	55–64	65 and over	65–74	75 and over
Total expenditures per consumer unit									
1990 $	28,381	16,525	28,117	35,594	37,012	29,263	18,551	20,901	15,450
1995 $	32,277	18,429	31,488	38,425	42,181	32,604	22,265	25,302	18,575
Health care expenditures per consumer unit									
1990 $	1,480	403	981	1,415	1,597	1,791	2,208	2,197	2,223
1995 $	1,732	465	1,096	1,609	1,850	1,909	2,647	2,617	2,683
Health care share of total expenditures per consumer unit									
1990	5.21%	2.44%	3.49%	3.98%	4.31%	6.12%	11.90%	10.51%	14.39%
1995	5.37%	2.52%	3.48%	4.19%	4.39%	5.86%	11.89%	10.34%	14.44%
Number of consumer units (in thousands)									
1990	96,968	7,581	21,287	21,003	14,855	12,162	20,079	11,318	8,761
1995	103,024	7,067	19,500	23,441	18,633	12,626	21,759	11,924	9,855
Share of consumer units by age of reference person									
1990	100.00%	7.81%	21.95%	21.66%	15.32%	12.54%	20.71%	11.67%	9.03%
1995	100.00%	6.86%	18.93%	22.75%	18.09%	12.26%	21.12%	11.57%	9.57%
Share of national health OOPs expenditures by age of reference person									
1990	100.00%	2.13%	14.55%	20.71%	16.53%	15.18%	30.87%	17.33%	13.57%
1995	100.00%	1.84%	11.98%	21.14%	19.32%	13.51%	32.28%	17.49%	14.82%

Source: United States Department of Labor, Bureau of Labor Statistics, *Consumer Expenditure Survey, 1990–91*, Table 12, and *Consumer Expenditure Survey, 1995*, Table 1300.

Table 2.3
Components of out-of-pocket health care expenditures by age group, United States, 1990 and 1995

Category	All consumers	Under 25	25–34	35–44	45–54	55–64	65 and over	65–74	75 and over
Total health care expenditures per consumer unit									
1990 $	1,480	403	981	1,415	1,597	1,791	2,208	2,197	2,223
1995 $	1,732	465	1,096	1,609	1,850	1,909	2,647	2,617	2,683
Health insurance									
1990 $	581	106	391	485	583	700	990	1,014	960
1995 $	860	209	517	726	817	896	1,541	1,528	1,557
1990 %	39.3	26.3	39.9	34.3	36.5	39.1	44.8	46.2	43.2
1995 %	49.6	44.9	47.2	45.1	44.2	46.9	58.2	58.4	58.0
Medical services									
1990 $	562	190	391	646	664	654	664	656	674
1995 $	511	157	380	596	664	587	479	471	487
1990 %	37.8	47.2	39.9	45.7	41.6	36.5	30.1	29.9	30.3
1995 %	29.5	33.8	34.7	37.0	35.9	30.8	18.1	18.0	18.2
Drugs (prescription and nonprescription)									
1990 $	252	65	135	183	236	340	475	455	501
1995 $	280	65	139	205	254	344	544	536	555
1990 %	17.0	16.1	13.8	12.9	14.8	19.0	21.5	20.7	22.5
1995 %	16.2	14.0	12.7	12.7	13.7	18.0	20.6	20.5	20.7
Medical supplies									
1990 $	85	41	64	100	113	96	80	73	88
1995 $	80	34	60	81	115	83	83	82	84
1990 %	5.7	10.2	6.5	7.1	7.1	5.4	3.6	3.3	4.0
1995 %	4.6	7.3	5.5	5.0	6.2	4.4	3.1	3.1	3.1

Source: See table 2.2.

Fourth, in a related development, the professional medical services component of OOP expenditures has fallen sharply since 1990, as insurers presumably have borne a greater share. In 1990, for example, the average expenditure on medical services by those aged 65 and over was $664, but by 1995 this had fallen 28% to $479. For all consumers, the medical service expenditure share fell from 38% to 30%, but for those 65 and over the drop was even larger, from 30% in 1990 to 18% in 1995.

Fifth, for drugs (the CES data include both prescription and over-the-counter nonprescription drug expenditures), in both 1990 and 1995 expenditures increased with age and were about twice as large for the elderly relative to all consumers. The level of OOP expenditures increased about 11% for all consumers from 1990 to 1995 ($252 to $280), but for the elderly, the OOPs increase was larger, about 14–15% ($475 to $544). In terms of expenditure shares, the drug component fell slightly, from 17% to 16% for all consumers, presumably reflecting a shift to payments by health insurers. For those 75 and over, the drop in the drug component of OOPs was slightly larger, from 22.5% in 1990 to 20.7% in 1995.

In summary, the CES data indicate that the composition of OOPs has changed considerably since 1990, and in different ways for the elderly versus the nonelderly. A dominant trend for people of all ages, however, is away from direct out-of-pocket payments for medical services, drugs, and medical supplies and instead toward health insurance. To the extent that this growth in health insurance results in greater buying power by agents of consumers relative to that of providers and suppliers, and to the extent any resulting lower provider-supplier prices are passed on to consumers in the form of lower health insurance premiums, this shift could result in benefits to consumers, particularly the elderly.

Medical Prices: Entire U.S. Population

Expenditures are by definition the product of price times quantity. Disaggregating the growth of health expenditures into price and quantity components involves many conceptual and practical difficulties.[8] The BLS publishes an aggregate medical care Consumer Price Index (MCPI) as well as price indexes for various of the MCPI components, such as prescription drugs, professional medical services, and hospital

---

8. For an overview discussion, see Triplett 1997 and Getzen 1992.

Table 2.4
Price inflation in the overall CPI and in the Medical CPI, 1927–1996, average annual growth rates

Time period	CPI-Urban	Medical CPI	Ratio MCPI/CPI
1927–46	0.60%	1.03%	1.72
1946–56	3.38%	4.22%	1.25
1956–66	1.76%	3.36%	1.91
1966–76	5.79%	7.05%	1.22
1976–86	6.78%	8.90%	1.31
1986–96	3.65%	6.46%	1.77
1927–96	3.24%	4.59%	1.42

Sources: U.S. Department of Labor, Bureau of Labor Statistics. For the MCPI prior to 1935, Langford 1957, Table 1, p. 1055.

and related services. Each of these price indexes is based on consumers' OOPs and thereby excludes all payments by governments and third-party insurers.[9]

Recent MCPI data show that prices consumers pay for medical care have been increasing more rapidly than those for other items. Indexed to 100 in 1990, the 1996 MCPI was 140.2, for prescription drugs it was 133.7, for nonprescription drugs and medical supplies 118.7, for physicians' services 134.6, and for hospital and related services 151.4, whereas the CPI for all items was only 120.0.[10] Thus, except for nonprescription drugs, prices of health-related items and services generally appear to have risen more rapidly than the overall CPI. Moreover, as table 2.4 shows, this more rapid increase of the MCPI relative to the CPI is not a recent phenomenon. Since 1927, the first year for which MCPI data are available, medical inflation has generally been greater than that of all goods and services.[11] Over the entire 1927–96 time period, the MCPI has risen at an AAGR of 4.59%, more than 40% above the 3.24% for the overall CPI.

In its recent report to the U.S. Senate Finance Committee (1996), however, the CPI commission concluded that the MCPI was substantially upward biased, stating that ". . . healthcare inflation is seriously

9. However, in constructing the BLS's MCPI, the out-of-pocket payments for health insurance are in turn distributed into payments by insurers for medical services, medical commodities, and health insurers' retained earnings. See Fixler 1996, Daugherty 1964, Ford and Sturm 1988, and Getzen 1992.
10. United States Department of Labor, Bureau of Labor Statistics, 1996, *CPI Detailed Report,* Tables 1 and 3 (CPI for All Urban Consumers).
11. For several years in 1927–46, however, year-to-year changes in the CPI were greater than for the MCPI. See Getzen 1992 for a discussion.

overstated because of the substantial uncounted quality change" (72, footnote 71), such as improvements in outcomes (60; see also Shapiro and Wilcox 1996). Specifically, the commission estimated that the upward bias of the MCPI is 3% per year for prescription drugs, for professional medical services, and for hospital and related services, and 1% for nonprescription drugs (58–62). Moreover, the commission recommended major changes in the BLS's treatment of health insurance expenditures (iv). Currently the BLS's procedures for the health insurance component do not take changing coverages into account, but instead simply multiply a medical care price index by an index of health insurance ex post retained earnings, that is, the ratio determined by health insurance revenues minus health insurance payments, all divided by health insurance revenues (Lane 1996, 22; see also references in note 9).

The BLS also publishes producer price indexes (PPIs) for various industries, focusing on the initial point in the distribution chain, where it "measures average changes in selling prices received by domestic producers for their output" (U.S. Department of Labor, Bureau of Labor Statistics 1992, 140). Although the BLS has published PPIs for certain health-related industries such as prescription pharmaceuticals for many years, currently there is no overall medical care PPI. Recently, however, the BLS introduced separate PPIs for offices and clinics of doctors of medicine (December 1993), skilled and intermediate care facilities (December 1994), general medical and surgical hospitals (December 1992), psychiatric hospitals (December 1992), and medical laboratories (June 1994). A number of recent research studies report that for pharmaceuticals, the PPI overstates price inflation considerably.[12] Studies by Cutler et al. (1996) on the treatment of heart attacks and by Shapiro and Wilcox (1996) on cataract surgery also suggest substantial upward bias in medical-related PPIs. Cutler et al. point out that apparent price inflation actually involves frequent substitution of more expensive but also more effective inputs.

Medical Prices: Focus on the Elderly

Larger medical-related expenditure weights for the elderly than for the young combined with apparent greater price inflation for medical care items than for the overall CPI has created an impression that the

---

12. See, for example, Berndt, Griliches, and Rosett 1993, Griliches and Cockburn 1994, and Berndt, Cockburn, and Griliches 1996.

relatively large price increases involving health care items and services in the last decade have adversely affected the elderly in particular. Indeed, such considerations played a prominent role in the recent debate concerning a possible downward adjustment of the CPI to index Social Security benefits for the elderly.[13] As noted earlier, however, the greater growth of the MCPI than for the CPI goes back at least to 1927. Hence, for the many years when today's elderly were younger, they too benefited from inflation that was less burdensome for them than for the elderly of their time. Over the entire life cycle, it is not at all clear whether today's elderly cohort is relatively better or worse off than earlier or future elderly cohorts. With this caveat in mind, along with the understanding that growth in the MCPI may be overstated because of overlooked quality improvements, we now briefly summarize the existing literature on separate price indexes for the elderly.[14]

Anticipating that the introduction of Medicare in July 1966 might have an impact on medical care prices in summer 1965 the Social Security Administration arranged with the BLS to collect supplementary prices for three surgical procedures—cholecystectomy (removal of gall bladder), prostatectomy (removal of prostate gland), and fractured neck of femur (hip surgery)—and two in-hospital medical services—acute myocardial infarction (treatment of heart attack) and cerebral hemorrhage (stroke)—that were particularly important to older persons, though not necessarily limited to them. A report to the President, summarized by Rice and Horowitz (1967, based on U.S. Department of Health, Education, and Welfare 1967), concluded that "[t]he index of the five in-hospital surgical and medical procedures particularly significant for the aged did not increase as rapidly during 1966 as the combined index for physicians' fees regularly priced for the CPI" (28).[15]

More recently, in response to a mandate from 1987 amendments to the Older Americans Act of 1965, the BLS created an experimental price index for elderly consumers (CPI-E). The CPI-E employs differential expenditure weights for the elderly (defined as ages 62 and over)

---

13. See, for example, Kuttner 1997 and Gephardt 1997.
14. For a review of literature on various BLS experimental price indexes, including a separate price index for the poor, both old and young, see Garner et al. 1996 and Moulton-Stewart 1997.
15. Rice and Horowitz (1967, 25) report that the December 1965–December 1966 price index growth rates ranged from 2.5% for cholecystectomy to 6.9% for prostatectomy, whereas the combined index for physicians' fees regularly priced for the CPI increased 7.8%.

and nonelderly, based on CES data, but assumes that within each category weight, the distribution of prices, the outlets from which consumers buy, the use of coupons and availability of discounts, as well as the quality of the items purchased, are the same for the elderly and the nonelderly.[16] From 1982 through 1996, the CPI-E for the elderly rose 67.9%, while the CPI rose 62.5%, implying that over the entire fourteen-year time span, the CPI had an AAGR of 3.53%, while the CPI-E for the elderly grew at a slightly larger 3.77% per year.[17] The larger health care expenditure weights for the elderly, along with greater measured medical price inflation, account almost entirely for the difference in AAGRs. As noted by the CPI commission, however, medical care prices are likely to have overstated inflation by not fully accounting for improvements in quality. If this is correct, then as Moulton and Stewart (1997) note, "A reduced rate of inflation for medical care would mitigate and perhaps eliminate any difference between the CPI-E and the official CPIs" (21).

A related recent study by Garner, Johnson, and Kokoski (1996) focuses on experimental price indexes for the poor, based on several alternative definitions of "poor." Using CES data for weights, along with CPI prices from 1984 to 1994, they find "very little difference between the experimental consumer price indexes produced for the poor and the corresponding CPI for the whole sample" (33). Similarly, Rubin and Koelin (1996), examining real income growth and expenditures on necessities for a variety of demographic groups from 1980 to 1990, conclude that

. . . for the population in general, well-being increased over the 1980s, as measured by both real income and discretionary spending. The well-being of elderly households increased relatively more than that of nonelderly households, and the well-being of recipients of cash assistance increased relatively less than that of those who did not receive assistance.[18] (P. 30)

In summarizing their findings concerning differential rates of price growth experienced by diverse groups in the population, the CPI commission stated:

Some have suggested that different groups in the population are likely to have faster or slower growth in their cost of living than recorded by changes in the

---

16. See Garner, Johnson, and Kokoski 1996, 37, and Moulton and Stewart 1997, 18. The time costs of shopping could also differ for the elderly.
17. See Amble and Stewart 1994 and Mason 1988. The overall CPI refers to the CPI-All Urban Consumers index.
18. Also see Hitschler 1993.

CPI. We find no compelling evidence of this to date. . . . Further work on this subject remains to be done. In particular, the prices actually paid, not just expenditure shares, may differ. (U.S. Senate Finance Committee 1996, 72)

With this information and brief overview of related literature as background, we now turn to a discussion of our own new research. In section III we focus on drug prices at the first point in the distribution chain, from producers to wholesalers, hospitals, and retailers.[19] In section IV we examine an intermediate point, namely, the acquisition prices retail pharmacies pay to wholesalers and manufacturers. Then in section V we assess prices at final points in the distribution chain, from retail pharmacies to patients and payors. Because of data limitations, we do not examine prices received by mail order pharmacies, which account for roughly 9% of total prescription dollar sales.

III. Producers' Prices for Drugs Destined for Use by Old versus Young

In reporting on prices at the first point in the distribution chain from manufacturers to wholesalers and retailers, the BLS publishes monthly PPIs for about fifty therapeutic classes of prescription pharmaceuticals, such as analgesics, broad- and medium-spectrum antibiotics, cancer therapy products, cardiovascular therapy products, antidepressants, and vitamins. Prices in these various therapeutic classes have increased at different rates. Since 1981, PPIs for anticoagulants, antiarthritics, and systemic anti-infectives, for example, have increased at much lower rates than have those for sedatives, central nervous system (CNS) stimulants/antiobesity preparations and psychotherapeutics.[20] Because the elderly are likely to have conditions, diseases, and illnesses that differ from those of the nonelderly, there is no a priori reason to expect that the price inflation for the basket of drugs used by the elderly has occurred at the same rate as that for the drug combinations used by the nonelderly.

IMS America, a firm specializing in sales and marketing data for medical and pharmaceutical products, regularly samples the prescrib-

---

19. In 1995 (1990), 78.9% (71.8%) of manufacturers' sales were to wholesalers, 12.1% (15.8%) were to retailers, and 4.8% (9.3%) were to hospitals (Pharmaceutical Research and Manufacturers of America 1997, fig. 4-12, p. 30).

20. Indexed to June 1981 = 100, the PPI index values in June 1996 were 145.9, 192.6, and 221.5 for anticoagulants, antiarthritics, and systemic anti-infectives, respectively and 730.9, 605.8, and 500.5 for sedatives, CNS stimulants/antiobesity preparations, and psychotherapeutics, respectively. (U.S. Department of Labor, Bureau of Labor Statistics, 1996, table 5, p. 61).

Table 2.5
Twenty top-selling market classes of prescription drugs, by age group, 1996

Under age 65 (81.3% of all mentions)

USC code	Class name	Mentions (thousands)	Percentage
15100	Broad- and medium-spectrum antibiotics	116,623	15.79
02200	Narcotic analgesics	40,955	5.55
64300	Antidepressants	34,623	4.69
09100	Systemic antiarthritics	32,446	4.39
52200	Plain corticoids	28,348	3.84
27100	Biological vaccines	26,593	3.60
28100	General bronchodilators	24,519	3.32
52100	Sex hormones	18,831	2.55
31400	Adrenergic blockers	16,753	2.27
64600	Antianxiety agents	16,611	2.25
31100	Antihypertensives	16,184	2.19
02100	Nonnarcotic analgesics	16,057	2.17
34300	Cough/cold preparation prescriptions	16,000	2.17
28400	Respiratory steroid inhalants	15,000	2.03
23400	Other antispasmodics	14,925	2.02
31700	Calcium channel blockers	14,876	2.01
37400	Fungicides alone/combination	11,993	1.62
34100	Oral cold preparation prescriptions	11,432	1.55
15500	Trimethoprim	11,374	1.54
33200	Oral contraceptives	11,203	1.52
	Sum for twenty leading market classes, under age 65	495,346	67.07

65 and over (18.7% of all mentions)

USC code	Class name	Mentions (thousands)	Percentage
15100	Broad- and medium-spectrum antibiotics	12,616	7.44
31100	Antihypertensives	10,718	6.32
31400	Adrenergic blockers	10,565	6.23
31700	Calcium channel blockers	10,479	6.18
41200	Noninjectable diuretics	8,736	5.15
02200	Narcotic analgesics	7,710	4.55
28100	General bronchodilators	7,268	4.29
09100	Systemic antiarthritics	6,874	4.05
52200	Plain corticoids	6,424	3.79
39200	Oral diabetes therapy	6,337	3.74
23400	Other antispasmodics	5,035	2.97
32100	Cholesterol reducers	4,918	2.90
31500	Digitalis preparations	4,037	2.38
64300	Antidepressants	3,987	2.35
31200	Vasodilators	3,694	2.18

Table 2.5 (continued)

USC code	Class name	Mentions (thousands)	Percentage
61600	Miotics plus glaucoma	3,433	2.02
30200	Other cancer/transplant cytotoxics	3,381	1.99
64600	Antianxiety agents	2,969	1.75
72100	Thyroid hormones	2,430	1.43
61400	Ophthalmic corticoids	2,362	1.39
Sum for twenty leading market classes, age 65 and over		123,973	73.10

Source: National Disease and Therapeutic Index (IMS America 1996).
Note: Data were also obtained and analyzed for 1994 and 1992 and yielded similar results.

ing behavior of office-based physicians and publishes the results in the *National Disease and Therapeutic Index* (NDTI). Based on an extensive sample of new prescriptions written by a panel consisting of about 3,000 physicians, information is gathered on, among other matters, patient age, physician specialty, physician age, diagnosis code, drug therapy prescribed, concomitant diagnoses, and desired actions; this sample NDTI data is then projected by IMS to national totals.[21]

NDTI data therefore permit us to compare the drugs prescribed for use by the elderly with those prescribed for younger patients, including differences involving brands versus generics. Based on annual NDTI data for 1996 we list, in the top panel of table 2.5, the twenty top-selling therapeutic classes of drugs for the elderly; in the bottom panel, we list the corresponding leading classes for the nonelderly. Prescriptions written for the elderly constitute 18.7% of all new prescriptions, whereas those for the nonelderly account for the remaining and much larger 81.3%. For both the young and the old, the leading therapeutic class is broad- and medium-spectrum antibiotics; drugs in this class comprise almost 15.8% of new prescriptions written for those under age 65, but only 7.4% for the elderly. The most frequent new prescriptions for the young include antidepressants, sex hormones, cough/cold preparations and oral contraceptives; those for the elderly include various cardiovasculars (antihypertensives, adrenergic blockers, calcium channel blockers, diuretics), as well as glaucoma and cancer therapies. The table does not consider differences between young and old in the relative use of drugs by therapeutic class; figure 2.1 highlights the most substantial of these differences. As the

21. For further details, see IMS America 1996, ch. 11. A new prescription refers to a new script written by the physician and is distinguished from continuing therapy.

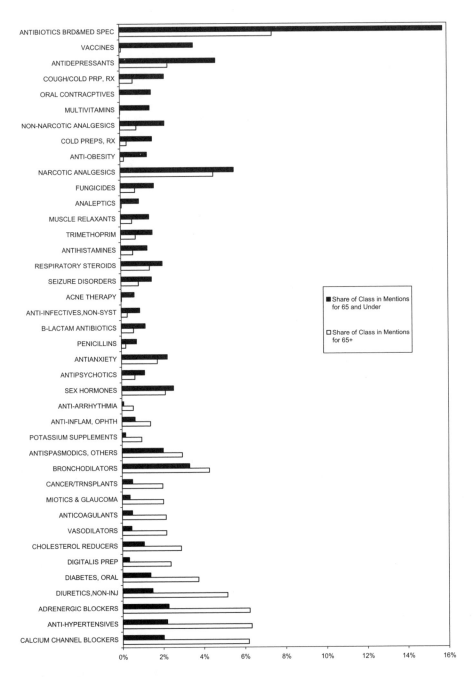

Figure 2.1
1996 NDTI drug mentions by age group and therapeutic class (largest differences between age groups)

figure shows, the five therapeutic classes with the largest differences in elderly-nonelderly usage are antibiotics, vaccines, antidepressants, cough and cold preparations, and oral contraceptives, all of which are more intensively used by the young.

We now turn to price data. The BLS makes publicly available the fixed-quantity weights it employs in aggregating the various therapeutic class-specific price indexes into an overall prescription pharmaceutical PPI. The third column of table 2.6 lists these quantity weights from the BLS's 1993 Cycle C sample; the next column lists the percentage of all new prescriptions in that therapeutic class that are written for the elderly. The final six columns list the BLS's PPI by therapeutic class annually from 1991 to 1996, normalized to 100.0 in 1990.

As shown in table 2.6, the elderly are particularly important consumers in a number of therapeutic classes—anticonvulsants (51%), cancer therapy products (39%), cardiovascular therapy products (42%), diabetes therapy (38%), diuretics (45%), and nutrients and supplements (53%)—although only for the cancer and cardiovascular therapy products are the PPI weights substantial. Therapeutic classes in which the elderly account for a relatively low fraction of consumption include systemic anti-infectives (10%), cough and cold preparations (7%), dermatological preparations (7%), muscle relaxants (8%), and vitamins (3%). Therapeutic classes with the largest price increases since 1990 include cough and cold preparations (57%), bronchial therapy (54%), anticonvulsants (48%), systemic antihistamines (45%), and psychotherapeutics (45%), and in all cases except anticonvulsants, these are therapeutic classes with disproportionately large to average use by the young, rather than by the elderly. Those therapeutic classes having the smallest price increases since 1990 include muscle relaxants (16%), ophthalmic and otic preparations (19%), miscellaneous prescription pharmaceuticals (21%), antiarthritics (22%), and vitamins (23%); these show a more mixed pattern of relative usage by old and young.

To aggregate these various therapeutic class PPIs into overall price indexes separately for the elderly and the nonelderly, we first assume, for the moment, that within each of the therapeutic classes old and young face the same prices (an assumption we relax in section IV) and multiply these BLS therapeutic class quantity weights by the relative old versus young proportions of 1996 new prescriptions, based on NDTI data. We then multiply these therapeutic class–specific elderly and nonelderly quantity weights times the BLS's published PPI for that

Table 2.6
BLS weights, elderly usage of prescription drugs, and producer price index by therapeutic class, 1990–1996

SIC code 2834-	Therapeutic class	PPI weight	Percentage elderly	BLS Producer Price Index (1990 = 100)					
				1991	1992	1993	1994	1995	1996
102	Analgesics	11,339	14	106.3	115.7	122.5	128.7	132.1	135.6
105	Antiarthritics	8,049	17	108.6	116.7	123.2	113.1	114.5	121.8
107	Anticonvulsants	2,100	51	112.7	125.9	132.7	136.8	142.1	148.3
109	Systemic antihistamines	9,336	13	111.7	121.3	126.5	131.4	135.7	145.4
111	Systemic anti-infectives	44,412	10	105.9	111.2	115.9	119.9	123.9	125.8
118	Bronchial therapy	11,956	19	111.2	122.5	129.0	139.6	145.8	154.2
119	Cancer therapies	10,079	39	106.0	116.6	120.8	123.4	127.7	132.7
121	Cardiovasculars	35,709	42	108.9	116.2	119.5	123.5	127.2	132.9
125	Cough and cold preparations	2,501	7	111.3	120.8	128.2	135.6	146.9	157.0
126	Dermatological preparations	5,237	7	104.8	111.8	118.8	124.2	133.5	140.5
127	Diabetes therapy	1,479	38	107.8	114.7	120.5	124.6	131.0	134.0
128	Diuretics	2,512	45	107.3	115.1	122.2	130.6	126.3	136.9
135	Hormones	13,047	17	108.7	116.3	122.9	133.5	137.8	137.3
139	Muscle relaxants	2,391	8	106.9	114.4	120.8	118.1	116.7	116.4
141	Nutrients and supplements	427	53	109.2	119.7	129.1	135.5	141.8	147.6
142	Ophthalmic and otic preparations	5,437	31	101.1	106.7	107.4	112.6	119.4	119.2
144	Psychotherapeutics	15,873	11	114.4	123.2	129.8	133.0	138.2	144.7
145	Sedatives	902	16	113.9	125.0	128.4	132.3	138.5	141.6
148	Vitamins	1,000	3	111.2	115.5	108.9	110.6	114.7	122.7
198	Miscellaneous pharmaceuticals	21,511	19	108.0	115.6	123.0	119.3	119.0	120.9

Notes: Percentage elderly is drug mentions for the elderly as a fraction of elderly plus nonelderly mentions. Drug mentions for age bracket not recorded in the NDTI are ignored. BLS PPIs for SIC 2834-116 (antispasmodic/antisecretory) and SIC 2834-147 (tuberculosis therapy) were not published from 1987 through 1993 and thus are ignored here; their elderly weights were 23 and 16, respectively, and their 1993 PPI weights were 11,956 and 1,607, respectively.

Table 2.7
Producer Price Indexes for all pharmaceuticals, those destined for use by the elderly, and those destined for use by the nonelderly

Year	Overall price index	Elderly price index	Nonelderly price index
1990	1.000	1.000	1.000
1991	1.083	1.083	1.083
1992	1.160	1.163	1.159
1993	1.213	1.211	1.213
1994	1.248	1.247	1.249
1995	1.287	1.284	1.288
1996	1.330	1.331	1.329

Note: See text for source and details of procedure for calculation.

class, normalized to unity in 1990.[22] Finally, we aggregate over the various therapeutic classes and thereby obtain separate prescription pharmaceutical PPIs for drugs destined for use by the elderly and the nonelderly. Table 2.7 summarizes results from this calculation over 1990–96.

The very striking conclusion that emerges from inspection of table 2.7 is that in aggregate, manufacturers' prices for pharmaceutical products destined for use by the elderly change at virtually the same rate as those destined for use by the nonelderly. By 1996, the PPI over all consumers was 1.330, that for the elderly was 1.331, and that for the nonelderly was 1.329. Hence, despite substantial differences in usage among the elderly and nonelderly of drugs from various therapeutic classes, and even though manufacturers' price changes since 1990 have varied considerably among the therapeutic classes, in the aggregate, at the initial point in the distribution chain from drug manufacturers, there appears to be no price inflation differential by age group, at least according to the official BLS price statistics.

IV. Retail Sell-In Prices: Elderly versus Nonelderly

The PPI calculations presented in the previous section assume that within each therapeutic class, prices for products destined for use by the elderly have the same distribution as those for the nonelderly. We now relax that assumption.

---

22. Notice that we are implicitly assuming here that the old-young distribution within each therapeutic class is the same for sales from manufacturers to wholesalers, to hospitals, and to retailers. We relax this assumption in section IV.

Based on its electronic computer record survey of about 34,000 retail pharmacies (independents, chains, mass merchandisers, and food stores), IMS gathers data on brand and generic sales for each chemical compound as well as on pharmacy acquisition prices and pharmacy selling prices for the highest selling form/strength/package of each product. In addition, IMS collects separate retail prices for the top-selling presentation of each product by method of payment—cash, Medicaid, and private third party. IMS reports these data in its *Retail Perspective* and its *Retail Methods of Payment.*[23]

Within each of these three therapeutic classes, data are therefore available on what drugs were prescribed, whether brand or generic, the leading selling form/strength/package of each product, whether destined for use by the elderly or the nonelderly, sell-in price to pharmacy, and sell-out prices to consumers and payors. Here we focus on that point in the distribution chain involving acquisition prices paid by retail pharmacies (what IMS calls sell-in prices), whereas in section V we focus on retail pharmacy sell-out prices to various consumers and payors. We now concentrate on three leading therapeutic classes: broad- and medium-spectrum antibiotics, calcium channel blockers, and antidepressants.

A priori, two possible hypotheses come to mind concerning differential elderly-nonelderly drug usage within these therapeutic classes. The first concerns medications used to treat acute conditions. It is plausible to assume that the health of seniors is more fragile than that of the nonelderly and that as a result, prudent medical practice would advise prescribing for the elderly those products that, given similar efficacy, had the fewest adverse interactions with other drugs and the fewest side effects.[24] Newly introduced drugs are frequently about as efficacious as older products but have superior adverse-interaction and side-effect profiles. More convenient dosing of newer products, such as once-a-day "sustained release" versions, also facilitates patient compliance, particularly for the elderly, who are more likely to have memory lapses. These newer products typically command a price premium and experience greater price inflation than older, off-patent generic drugs.[25] To the extent these assumptions are valid, therefore, we would hypothesize that for medications used to treat acute condi-

---

23. For further details, see IMS America 1996, chaps. 20 and 41.

24. One might also argue that the very young are more vulnerable as well.

25. This is clearly the case for antidepressants, such as the selective serotonin reuptake inhibitors, which have similar efficacy but superior adverse-interaction and side-effect

tions, prices faced by the elderly would tend to grow more rapidly than those for the young.[26]

A second hypothesis concerns medications used to treat chronic conditions. Here the same basic factors are at work as noted above for acute conditions. In addition, however, for chronic conditions, the old might be expected to have chosen to use older drug products, for physicians are hesitant to change medications when a particular existing drug regimen is working well.[27] With stickier consumption patterns and by surviving to old age, the elderly would therefore disproportionally use older drugs, which are more often available as generics. If this hypothesis is true, drug prices within certain chronic areas might grow less rapidly for the elderly versus the nonelderly, because generic prices have fallen in the last decade while prices of brands typically increased. (See, for example, Griliches and Cockburn 1994 and Berndt, Cockburn, and Griliches 1996.)

However, patent protection has expired for only the *very* old drugs. For older drugs still patent protected, price increases tend to be larger than for younger drugs. (See, for example, Berndt, Griliches, and Rosett 1993; Kanoza 1996; and Ristow 1996.) Thus, any price inflation differential between old and young consumers of both acute and chronic medications depends on the distribution of sales between older drugs with and without patent protection. Because such a distribution is an empirical matter that could vary by therapeutic class and change over time, our hypotheses make no definitive prediction for any elderly-nonelderly price inflation differential but must be examined in the context of the distribution of sales between brands and generics in each therapeutic class.

Among the three therapeutic classes we examine here, we expect that the cardiovascular products, such as calcium channel blockers, are used predominantly for treatment of chronic conditions, whereas the broad- and medium-spectrum antibiotics are used primarily to treat acute conditions. In terms of protracted use, antidepressants are most likely to fall between the antibiotics and the cardiovasculars, because they are used to treat both episodic and more chronic forms of depression. In all three therapeutic classes, however, the elderly and

profiles relative to the older tricyclic antidepressants. See Berndt, Cockburn, and Griliches 1996 for further discussion.

26. For a discussion of pricing considerations involving drugs to treat acute versus chronic conditions, see Lu and Comanor 1996.

27. This is consistent with the common medical adage, "Don't shoot a singing bird."

nonelderly may use drugs for a different set of conditions. In the case of antidepressants, for example, physicians frequently prescribe tricyclic antidepressants for "off-label" conditions, such as chronic pain syndromes, that the elderly experience more frequently.

With this as background, we begin by examining retail pharmacy acquisition (sell-in) costs and price indexes for the broad- and medium-spectrum antibiotic (AB) class of drugs. As the top panel of table 2.8 shows, retail acquisitions of ABs almost doubled from 1990 to 1996, growing from $2.1 to $3.8 billion. Roughly 90% of the retail pharmacy acquisition costs are for ABs destined for use by the young. The overall brand/generic shares for ABs are somewhat volatile, ranging from 81%/19% in 1990 to 90%/10% in 1993. Over the entire time period, brand share for the elderly has grown from 82% to 91% (generic share has fallen from 18% to 9%), whereas for the young, the brand share has increased only from 81% to 87%. The AB brand share hit its peak in 1992–94 at about 89–90% (for all), then fell to about 88% (all), 87% (young) and 91% (elderly) in 1996. Thus, particularly since 1992–94, the elderly's use of branded antibiotic products has grown considerably more rapidly and to greater proportions than that of the young. This is, of course, consistent with the acute-care hypothesis discussed above. It is also consistent with the notion that the elderly are increasingly using newer, branded products having higher efficacy in treating severe or life-threatening infections such as pneumonia, in part because of increasing bacterial resistance to older drugs.[28]

We now turn to price indexes, which can be constructed in a number of ways. The BLS employs a fixed-weight procedure known as the Laspeyres price index that keeps weights of the various items in the index fixed over time. The CPI commission has criticized this fixed-weight procedure and has recommended instead a chain-weighted index with changing weights that reflect evolving market shares of items over time. (See U.S. Finance Committee 1996.) The most common version of such a chained index is the (Tornqvist discrete approximation to the) Divisia index.[29] We therefore construct price indexes mim-

---

28. Successful brands introduced since 1990 with substantial use by the elderly include Floxin and Lorabid. Sales of other, older brands such as Ceftin and Cipro (introduced in 1987) have also grown substantially.

29. The fixed-weight Laspeyres price index is calculated as $L_t \equiv \Sigma_i p_{it} q_{i0} / \Sigma_i p_{i0} q_{i0}$, where p_{it} is the price of item i in period t, p_{i0} is the base period price, and q_{i0} is the base period quantity. The Tornqvist discrete approximation to the Divisia index is calculated as $D_t \equiv \exp[\varpi_{it}(\ln p_{it} - \ln p_{i,t-1})] \cdot D_{t-1}$, where $\varpi_{it} \equiv .5*(\omega_{it} + \omega_{i,t-1})$ and $\omega_{it} \equiv p_{it} q_{it} / \Sigma_i p_{it} q_{it}$, and were D_0 is normalized to unity in the base year.

icking the BLS fixed-weight procedure, using 1990 fixed-quantity weights, but also report price indexes with the more preferred Divisia index calculation that allows for changing market shares.[30]

In rows labeled "Laspeyres" in the top panel of table 2.8, we present 1990–96 retail acquisition price indexes for ABs over all consumers (Laspeyres index—All), for ABs destined for use by the young (Young) and for ABs destined for use by the old (Elderly).[31] We first obtain the somewhat surprising result that with the Laspeyres index, over the entire 1990–96 time period, ABs used by the elderly increased in price about 12%, whereas for the nonelderly the price increase was somewhat larger, at 17%. However, if one looks only from 1992 onward, the reverse occurred—the elderly AB price index increased 11%, from 1.009 to 1.121, whereas that for the nonelderly increased 7%, from 1.096 to 1.173.

These findings for ABs are essentially unaffected when one employs changing share weights and the preferable Divisia index.[32] As seen in the bottom three rows of the top panel of table 2.8 and graphically in figure 2.2, using the Divisia, by 1996 the price index for ABs destined for use by the elderly was 1.07, slightly less than the 1.11 for the young. After 1992, however, the AB price index increased only very slightly for the young (2% from 1.08 in 1992 to 1.11 in 1996), whereas for the elderly it increased considerably more (7%, from 1.00 to 1.07). In part, this old-young differential reflects a greater increase in use of newer branded drugs by the old than by the young since 1992, as noted above. To show this in greater detail, in figure 2.3 we present 1996 elderly utilization for each AB molecule and distinguish brands (light bars) from multisource (dark bars) drugs. The dotted vertical line in figure 2.3 represents the elderly average percentage over all ABs (9.8%). The elderly's differential use of brands and generics can be seen by noting that for the vast majority of drugs involving relatively

---

30. This fixed-weight procedure is not the same as that employed by the BLS in its CPI for prescription drugs for a number of reasons, including the fact that the CPI uses only OOPs' weights, whereas weights here include retail acquisition costs for products destined for payment by cash, third party and Medicaid. Moreover, the index here refers to retail acquisition costs, not retail sales to patients and payors. Cleeton, Goepfrich, and Weisbrod (1992) and Armknecht, Moulton, and Stewart (1994) describe the BLS's CPI method for prescription drugs.
31. The elderly-nonelderly split for each drug is based on the average of the 1992, 1994, and 1996 NDTI values.
32. For the Laspeyres, the number of AB items is fixed at 156, whereas for the Divisia, the numbers are 162, 172, 188, 188, 190, 192, and 196, respectively, from 1990 to 1996.

Table 2.8
Retail pharmacy acquisition (sell-in) costs and price indexes by therapeutic class, 1990–1996

Class/Category	1990	1991	1992	1993	1994	1995	1996
Antibiotics—Broad- and medium-spectrum							
Total drug costs (thousands)	$2,094,060	$2,527,380	$2,839,640	$3,274,900	$3,422,040	$3,791,320	$3,767,950
Share—Young	.891	.890	.888	.889	.885	.881	.875
Share—Elderly	.109	.110	.112	.111	.115	.119	.125
Share—Brand—All	.814	.846	.892	.897	.894	.833	.879
Share—Generic—All	.186	.154	.108	.103	.106	.167	.121
Young	.187	.156	.110	.105	.109	.173	.126
Elderly	.175	.141	.094	.088	.088	.120	.088
Laspeyres index—All	1.000	1.055	1.087	1.125	1.132	1.096	1.167
Young	1.000	1.055	1.096	1.135	1.141	1.103	1.173
Elderly	1.000	1.056	1.009	1.040	1.060	1.043	1.121
Divisia index—All	1.000	1.055	1.073	1.101	1.112	1.117	1.106
Young	1.000	1.055	1.083	1.112	1.121	1.125	1.109
Elderly	1.000	1.055	0.995	1.020	1.038	1.056	1.072
Antidepressants							
Total drug costs (thousands)	$940,460	$1,047,720	$1,402,000	$1,715,030	$2,396,310	$3,064,150	$3,730,927
Share—Young	.899	.899	.901	.904	.909	.910	.911
Share—Elderly	.101	.101	.099	.096	.091	.090	.089
Share—Brand—All	.882	.899	.905	.893	.935	.956	.970
Share—Generic—All	.118	.101	.095	.107	.065	.044	.029
Young	.115	.098	.090	.100	.061	.041	.028
Elderly	.149	.126	.138	.176	.110	.073	.048

Laspeyres index—All	1.000	1.077	1.176	1.208	1.228	1.267	1.320
Young	1.000	1.077	1.176	1.209	1.230	1.269	1.321
Elderly	1.000	1.074	1.168	1.200	1.209	1.247	1.304
Divisia index—All	1.000	1.077	1.168	1.187	1.190	1.217	1.272
Young	1.000	1.077	1.169	1.189	1.195	1.224	1.279
Elderly	1.000	1.076	1.161	1.172	1.145	1.158	1.201
Calcium Channel Blockers							
Total drug costs (thousands)	$1,697,136	$2,068,896	$2,597,408	$2,821,445	$3,061,874	$3,146,177	$3,179,213
Share—Young	.546	.560	.566	.575	.577	.580	.585
Share—Elderly	.454	.440	.434	.425	.423	.420	.415
Share—Brand—All	.985	.973	.973	.928	.921	.936	.955
Share—Generic—All	.015	.027	.027	.072	.079	.064	.045
Young	.015	.034	.032	.072	.077	.062	.046
Elderly	.014	.018	.021	.072	.082	.068	.045
Laspeyres index—All	1.072	1.072	1.135	1.178	1.197	1.234	1.267
Young	1.072	1.072	1.134	1.175	1.192	1.229	1.261
Elderly	1.072	1.072	1.136	1.181	1.203	1.242	1.273
Divisia index—All	1.061	1.061	1.105	1.132	1.087	1.098	1.105
Young	1.061	1.061	1.103	1.130	1.082	1.093	1.100
Elderly	1.061	1.061	1.108	1.135	1.094	1.105	1.111

Notes: Laspeyres index employs fixed 1990 weights. See text discussion for sources.

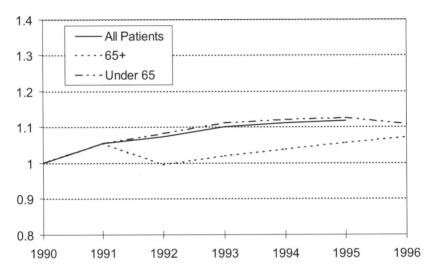

Figure 2.2
Divisia price indexes for antibiotics ("sell in" prices to retail pharmacies)
Source: IMS *Retail Audit*, IMS *NDTI*, authors' calculations.

intense use by the elderly, the molecule in question is a branded, single-source (light bar) drug.

We now turn to retail sell-in prices for antidepressants (ADs). As the top row of the middle panel of table 2.8 shows, retail-sector purchases of ADs surged by a factor of about four between 1990 and 1996, thereby growing considerably more rapidly than those of ABs, although by 1996 total retail acquisition expenditures for the two were about equal, at $3.73 billion for ADs versus $3.77 billion for ABs. ADs were also similar to ABs in that the retail acquisition dollar share for products destined for use by the young for both classes was about 90%, with a very slight upward trend over the period. A distinctive feature of the AD market involves the tremendous growth in sales of the newest generation of ADs, the selective serotonin reuptake inhibitors (SSRIs) such as Prozac, Zoloft, Paxil, Luvox, and Serzone. This high growth of new branded products has resulted in a sharply declining generic dollar share of retail-sector purchases (from 12% in 1990 to 3% in 1996) and a corresponding increase in the dollar share for brands (88% to 97%). In each year between 1990 and 1996, the share of retail drugstore purchases of generic ADs for use by the elderly was larger than that for the young; the 1990 generic shares for old and young were 15% and 12%, respectively, and by 1996 they had fallen to 5% and 3%, respec-

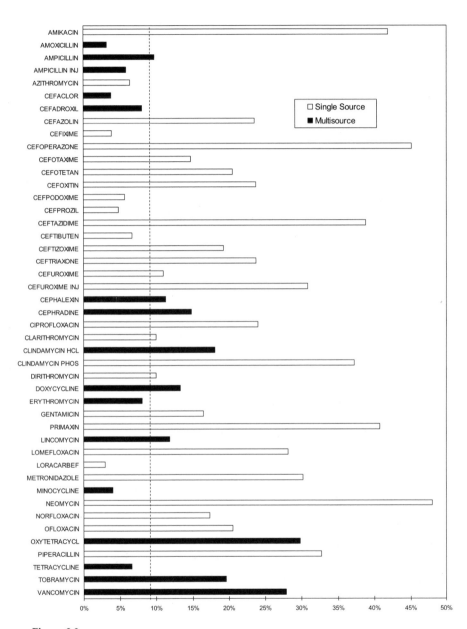

Figure 2.3
Share of 1996 NDTI mentions for age 65+ patients: Antibiotics
Source: IMS *NDTI* and authors' calculations.

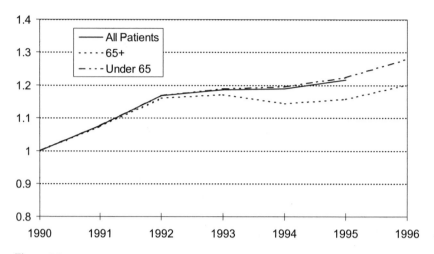

Figure 2.4
Divisia price indexes for antidepressants ("sell in" prices to retail pharmacies)
Source: IMS *Retail Audit*, IMS *NDTI*, authors' calculations.

tively. This differential brand-generic pattern could reflect the phenomenon noted above that certain generic tricyclic antidepressants are often prescribed "off-label" to treat chronic pain syndromes that occur more frequently in the elderly.

With respect to price indexes, we first report results based on the fixed-weight Laspeyres procedure. As shown in the middle panel of table 2.8, the AD price inflation differential between old and young appears to be negligible—by 1996, the Laspeyres index for the elderly was 1.30, very slightly less than that for the young at 1.32.

For the more appropriate Divisia index, which takes changing shares into account, however, the inflation differential is considerably larger, with the 1996 index being 1.20 for the elderly but 1.28 for the young.[33] In figure 2.4 we plot these Divisia AD price indexes for the entire population, for the elderly, and for the young. As the figure shows, price inflation for retail acquisitions of ADs destined for use by the elderly has been appreciably less than that for ADs destined for use by the young.

To understand the reason underlying this inflation differential, in figure 2.5 we plot the elderly share for each AD chemical molecule; the patent-protected drugs are again marked with light bars, and generic

---

33. The number of items in the 1990 fixed weight Laspeyres index is 46, whereas for the Divisia it is 50 in 1990–1, 54 in 1992–3, 58 in 1994–5, and 60 in 1996.

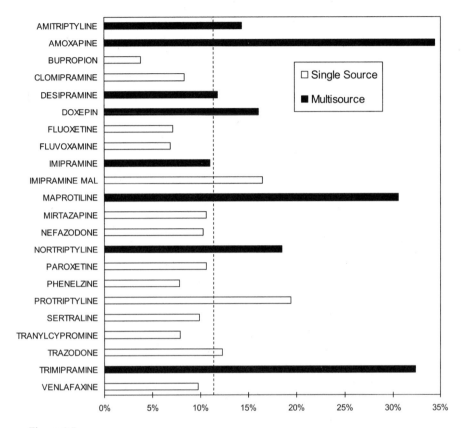

Figure 2.5
Share of 1996 NDTI mentions for age 65+ patients: Antidepressants
Source: IMS *NDTI* and authors' calculations.

or multisource drugs are marked with dark bars; over all AD molecules, the elderly average share is 10.3%, represented by the dotted vertical line. As the figure shows, the elderly's use of off-patent and generic drugs such as trimipramine, protriptyline, nortriptyline, maprotiline, imipramine, doxepin, amoxapine, and amitriptyline is above that of the general population. Elderly use of some newer and still patent-protected branded drugs such as venlafaxine (brand name Effexor), sertraline (Zoloft), paroxetine (Paxil), and nefazodone (Serzone) is about the same as that of the general population, but elderly use of other patent-protected ADs such as fluvoxamine (Luvox), fluoxetine (Prozac), and buproprion (Wellbutrin) is less than that by the general population. Given these differential brand-generic uses by the elderly versus the young, and with generic prices falling while brand prices are increasing, the basket of ADs destined for use by the elderly is increasing more slowly in price than the basket of ADs destined for use by the young. Because it employs changing share rather than fixed weights, the Divisia index better captures these dynamics. Note that the inflation differential would be even larger if the dollar share of generics had not been falling.

Next we turn to the calcium channel blockers (CCBs), drugs used to treat cardiovascular conditions, which have brand names such as Cardizem, Norvasc, and Procardia XL. As with the ABs, acquisition costs of CCBs among retailers approximately doubled from 1990 to 1996, with total acquisition costs of around $3.2 billion in 1996, about 15% less than for ABs. The elderly share of CCBs, however, is much larger than that for ABs and ADs. As the bottom panel of table 2.8 shows, the retail acquisition dollar share of CCBs for the elderly is more than 40%, having fallen slightly from 45% in 1990 to 42% in 1996. The brand-generic market share pattern is also different, and is not monotonic over time, reflecting in part episodic patent expirations and generic entry within the 1990–96 time frame. For the elderly, the generic share increased from 1% in 1990 to 8% in 1994, then fell to about 4% in 1996; for the young, the respective generic shares are similar, at 2%, 8%, and 4% for those same years, respectively.

In terms of price indexes, because of the relatively small brand-generic differences by age group, there is only a negligible difference between CCB retail-acquisition price inflation for products destined for use by the elderly versus those for the young. Specifically, as shown in the bottom panel of table 2.8 and graphically in figure 2.6, the old-young Laspeyres indexes are 1.27 versus 1.26, whereas for the Divisia they are 1.11 versus 1.10. In large part, this similarity in elderly-nonelderly price inflation for CCBs reflects the fact that brand-generic differences between the old and young are much smaller in any given year for the CCBs than they are for the ADs and ABs. Figure 2.7 displays this more modest relative variability for each of the CCB chemical molecules. Variations in elderly-nonelderly differences, other than for bepridil (brand name Vascor) and nimodipine (Nimotop), are modest.

In summary, therefore, over the entire 1990–96 time period, retail-acquisition price inflation for antidepressants destined for use by the elderly has been less than that for the young, reflecting the elderly's greater use of generic antidepressants. Price inflation has been consid-

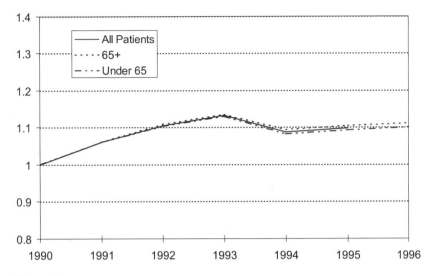

Figure 2.6
Divisia price indexes for calcium channel blockers ("sell in" prices to retail pharmacies)
Source: IMS *Retail Audit*, IMS *NDTI*, authors' calculations.

erably greater since 1992 for antibiotics used by the elderly, but the differential is much smaller over the entire 1990–96 time period. Moreover, for antibiotics, the greater elderly price inflation since 1992 appears to reflect the more rapid growth in the elderly's use of the newest, branded drugs, for which bacterial resistance is less. For calcium channel blockers, however, the elderly-nonelderly inflation differentials are negligible.

Two other general results are worth noting. First, growth over time in the sell-in prices for all three therapeutic classes based on the IMS data employed here is less than the inflation as measured by the BLS's producer price index, even when employing the Laspeyres procedure; the 1990–96 differences here are 1.29% per year for ABs, 1.61% for ADs, and 0.83% for CCBs.[34] This differential could reflect different pricing for leading (best-selling) presentations of drugs (the IMS data) than for the basket examined by the BLS, but it could also reflect a known BLS bias in oversampling older branded drugs. (For further discussion, see

---

34. These differences are computed as growth in the BLS's PPI by therapeutic class (systemic anti-infectives for ABs, psychotherapeutics for ADs, and cardiovasculars for CCBs), reported in table 2.6, minus growth in the Laspeyres index—All entries of table 2.8.

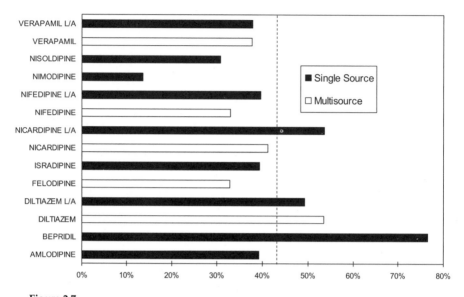

Figure 2.7
Share of 1996 NDTI mentions for age 65+ patients: Calcium channel blockers
Source: IMS *NDTI* and authors' calculations.

Berndt, Cockburn, and Griliches 1996; Berndt, Griliches, and Rosett 1993; IMS America 1996; and Kanoza 1996.)

Secondly, as shown in table 2.8, in each case the fixed-weight Laspeyres price index yields a larger measure of price inflation than does the corresponding Divisia index. Over all consumers, for example, the difference is 0.92% per year for ABs, 0.65% for ADs, and 2.34% for CCBs. If one sums these two differentials, the differences in average annual growth rates between the BLS's PPI and the Divisia for retail acquisition prices is 2.21% for ABs, 2.26% for ADs and 3.17% for CCBs. These results are therefore quite consistent with other findings reported by the CPI commission and emphasize the importance of the recommendations the commission made, particularly those involving use of changing versus fixed weights.

V. Retail Sell-Out Prices: Elderly Versus Nonelderly

We now examine price growth in the final point of the distribution chain, that from retail pharmacies to patients and payors. Our research here must be viewed as preliminary in at least two respects. First, we have been unable to obtain reliable method-of-payment data that separates cash, Medicaid, and third-party insurance payment for the elderly and the nonelderly since 1991. Data graciously made available to us involving a third-party insurer implied an implausibly huge decline in the elderly's use of cash as a method of payment. Our inability to obtain reliable national data is unfortunate, for casual empiricism suggests to us that the elderly's use of third-party payment arrangements to pay for drugs has increased more rapidly in the last few years than that of the general population, particularly because the retired have moved into "Medigap" managed-care arrangements that offer prescription drug benefits. If in fact in recent years seniors have moved to third-party drug payment more rapidly than the young (consistent with the OOPs data in table 2.3) and therefore increasingly are less affected by higher cash prices, then seniors are disproportionately availing themselves of lower managed-care prices, resulting in lower drug price inflation (but perhaps still higher average price levels) than that experienced by the nonelderly. Research on this issue must be postponed until appropriate data become available.

Second, the IMS sell-out methods-of-payment data are based on the best-selling presentation of a particular branded or generic drug. Problems emerge in measuring price and quantity changes consistently over time when these leading presentations change for brands, and even more so for specific generic manufacturers, over the time period under consideration. These problems are particularly evident in our data involving the antibiotics and calcium channel blockers, as are related problems involving products embodying combinations of chemical molecules. In the future we will be working with IMS to obtain data on additional presentations for branded and generic chemical molecules as well as information involving the combination products.

For antidepressants, fortuitously, this second problem involving leading presentations turns out essentially not to be an issue. Thus we report here our preliminary findings on sell-out prices by retail pharmacies for only the antidepressant class of prescription drugs. Moreover, because reliable method-of-payment data distinguishing among cash, Medicaid, and third party are not yet available for the elderly and the nonelderly, here we simply employ a weighted average of prices among the three payment methods, assuming the weights in table 2.1 to be the same for the elderly and nonelderly.

IMS method-of-payment data are available only since 1991, whereas the sell-in data analyzed in the previous section go back to 1990. We therefore begin by renormalizing the AD sell-in data from table 2.8 so that the Divisia price index for the AD drugs is 1.000 in 1991. The upper left panel of table 2.9 presents the results of that renormalization. As the table shows, from 1991 to 1996, sell-in prices for AD drugs destined for use by the elderly increased 12%, whereas sell-in prices for AD drugs destined for use by the young increased 19%.

In the introduction to this chapter, we noted the dramatic change over time in retail methods of payment, away from cash and toward third-party payor. For retail pharmacies, the growth in third-party payment implies dealing with a more organized and powerful buyer/payor than is the typical cash customer. We therefore expect that over this time period, sell-out prices (the sum of copayments and third-party reimbursements received by the retail pharmacies) have increased less rapidly than have sell-in prices. One very simple way of highlighting this difference is to compute a "gross margin index," defined as the sell-out price index divided by the sell-in price index, the former incorporating data from table 2.1 on changing methods of payment over time, assumed to be the same for ADs as for all drugs.

In the top right panel of table 2.9, we present the Divisia price index for retail sell-out, normalized to unity in 1991, and in the bottom panel we list the gross margin index, constructed as outlined in the previous paragraph. Two results are particularly interesting.

First, as expected, the increased role of third-party payors since 1991 has pressured pricing downward in the retail pharmacy sector; although AD prices on a sell-in basis increased 18% over all customers from 1991 to 1996, corresponding sell-out prices increased only 14%. Thus, gross margins for retail pharmacies selling AD products fell 3.5% from 1991 to 1996.

Second, this declining gross margin primarily involved sales of ADs to the young, for whom sell-in retail acquisition prices increased 18.8% from 1991 to 1996 while sell-out prices increased 14.2%, implying a decline of 3.8% in gross margins. For the elderly, however, the gross margin hardly declined at all; indeed, it increased very slightly, 0.4%.

One reason for this disparity is that, as noted earlier and shown visually in figure 2.5, the elderly are disproportionately large consumers of generic AD drugs. A number of studies have documented that the retail gross margin on generic drugs is larger, not only in percent-

Table 2.9
Divisia retail sell-in and sell-out price indexes for antidepressants

Year	Sell-in Divisia price index			Sell-out Divisia price index		
	Young	Elderly	Total	Young	Elderly	Total
1991	1.000	1.000	1.000	1.000	1.000	1.000
1992	1.085	1.079	1.084	1.075	1.073	1.075
1993	1.104	1.089	1.102	1.083	1.076	1.082
1994	1.110	1.064	1.105	1.081	1.073	1.080
1995	1.136	1.076	1.130	1.114	1.096	1.112
1996	1.188	1.116	1.181	1.142	1.121	1.140

Gross margin index (Sell-out/Sell-in)			
Year	Young	Elderly	Total
1991	1.000	1.000	1.000
1992	0.990	0.994	0.992
1993	0.981	0.988	0.982
1994	0.974	1.008	0.977
1995	0.980	1.018	0.984
1996	0.962	1.004	0.965

Note: Sell-out is in dollars per daily dose of leading presentation, weighted average over channels, with the same channel weights for old and young.

age terms, but often also in absolute amounts, than that on branded products (see, for example, the Federal Trade Commission study by Masson and Steiner (1985) as well as Caves, Whinston, and Hurwitz 1991); that turns out to be the case here as well.[35] One implication of this larger generic retail margin along with disproportionately large elderly use of generics is that retail pharmacy margins have been under greater downward pressure from nonelderly customers than from the elderly. It must be emphasized, however, that these calculations in table 2.9 assume that the method-of-payment trends displayed in table 2.1 are the same for ADs as over all drugs, and the same for the elderly and the young. If in fact the elderly are moving into

35. For one well-known branded selective serotonin reuptake inhibitor, for example, the sell-in price in 1996 was $1.71, but the sell-out price averaged over method-of-payment channel was $2.06, implying a $0.35 absolute margin and a 20.5% percentage gross margin [(sell-out/sell-in) −1]. By comparison, for one well-known older generation tricyclic antidepressant, the sell-in price was $0.12, and the sell-out price was $0.54, implying a $0.42 absolute margin and a 350% percentage gross margin. Note that one would expect the percentage margin to be larger for generics, because a common dispensing fee is added to a lower generic acquisition price.

third-party payment arrangements for drugs more rapidly than the young, these gross margin differentials between young and old tend to be overstated.

VI. Summary and Issues for Further Research

Our purpose in this chapter has been to examine whether prescription drug price inflation in the 1990s has differed between the elderly and the nonelderly when prices are viewed at three alternative points in the distribution chain. Our first finding is that in the aggregate, over all therapeutic classes of prescription drugs, we find essentially no age-related price inflation differential at the initial point in the distribution chain involving manufacturers' sales to wholesalers, retailers, and hospitals.

At an intermediate point in the distribution chain involving acquisition prices of retail pharmacies for purchases from manufacturers and wholesalers, we examined sell-in prices for three therapeutic classes of pharmaceuticals, antidepressants, antibiotics and calcium channel blockers over 1990–96. Here we observed some elderly-young price inflation differentials. Specifically, we found that from 1990 to 1996, the Divisia price index for ADs destined for use by the elderly grew at an average annual growth rate (AAGR) of 3.10%, whereas that for ADs destined for use by the young grew at a higher AAGR of 4.19%. The source of the elderly's lower inflation rate was their disproportionately greater use of older and generic drugs, whose prices are typically falling, whereas those of newer and branded ADs are generally increasing.

For ABs, we observed a slightly different set of trends. Over the entire 1990–96 time period, the Divisia price index for ABs destined for use by the elderly grew at an AAGR of 1.17%, again somewhat less than the 1.74% for those destined for use by the young. Since 1992, however, the elderly price index for ABs has grown at an AAGR of 1.88%, considerably more than the 0.59% for the nonelderly. This difference appears to arise from a more rapid growth among the elderly in the use of the newer, branded drugs than among the young, particularly since 1992. One interpretation of this apparent price inflation differential is that the more fragile elderly are disproportionately using the newer antibiotics that have not yet developed bacterial resistance, when being treated for severe or life-threatening infections such as pneumonia.

Finally, for the calcium channel blockers, the elderly-young sell-in price inflation differential was found to be negligible, with AAGRs being 1.60% for the young and 1.77% for the elderly.

The final point we examined in the distribution chain involves sales of retail pharmacies to consumers and payors. Because of data limitations, we were able to compute sell-out price indexes only for the antidepressant class of prescription drugs. The dramatically increasing share of prescriptions paid for by third-party insurance since 1991 has resulted in retail pharmacy sell-out prices for ADs increasing less rapidly than sell-in prices. The retail pharmacy gross margin index over all customers appears to have fallen about 3.5% between 1991 and 1996, with young patients enjoying most of the benefits of this increased power of managed care over time at the expense of the retail pharmacy sector. For the elderly, the retail gross margin on ADs has not fallen—indeed it has risen very slightly, reflecting in part the fact that the elderly are disproportionately large users of generic ADs, along with the previously documented finding that retail margins on generics tend to be larger than those on branded products. Our sell-out and gross margin calculations assume that trends in methods of payment among cash, Medicaid, and third-party payors are the same for the elderly and the young. To the extent that recently the elderly are enrolling in third-party arrangements with drug benefits at a more rapid rate than the young, this gross margin differential tends to be overstated, as does growth in sell-out prices for the elderly.

One useful extension of our empirical analysis would involve the introduction of mail-order data into our analysis. Although mail-order sales currently account for only about 9% of all prescription drug sales dollars, mail order is a rapidly growing segment, and apparently one in which the elderly are disproportionately represented.[36] Excluding mail-order prescription drug sales from our analysis most likely results in our overstating overall price growth for the elderly.

In this chapter we have made no attempt to adjust estimated price inflation differentials for variations in the quality of the products used by the elderly versus the young, nor have we linked prices of generics at entry with previous prices of their patented antecedents. It is possible, of course, that our findings on greater elderly AB price inflation relative to the young and smaller elderly AD price inflation when

---

36. Data made available to us involving one mail-order firm showed that more than half the prescriptions it dispensed were mailed to patients 65 years and older.

compared to the young could be entirely reversed were quality adjustments taken into account. Adjusting price changes and price differentials for quality changes is therefore an important issue meriting
further research.

One clear finding emerging from this research and corroborated in
other studies cited by the CPI commission is that the use of a fixed-
weight Laspeyres price index procedure, such as that employed by the
BLS, yields price indexes whose growth is misleading and distorted. In
particular, for all three classes of drugs studied, and for all groups of
customers, price growth as measured by the Laspeyres fixed-weight
procedure (as employed by the BLS) resulted in greater measured
inflation than the market share chain-weighted Divisia index. This
finding is consistent with that of other studies cited in the CPI commission's report and emphasizes the importance of their finding concerning the upward bias of the Laspeyres index and their recommendation
of moving to a changing-weight index.

Finally, in this chapter we have examined inflation price differentials
involving the elderly and the nonelderly, implicitly assuming that the
elderly are homogeneous. It is possible, of course, that there are more
differences within the elderly than there are between the elderly and
the young. Is income or expenditure inequality greater among the
elderly than between the young and elderly? Are there more children
living in poverty than there are elderly living solely on Social Security?
Clearly, formulating appropriate public policy involving the elderly
depends in part on the within versus between issue involving the
elderly.[37] In a somewhat different context involving other products,
Robert Michael (1979) reports greater variation in expenditures within
various demographic groups than between them. Examining the variability in health expenditures and in price inflation for health-related
items within the elderly demographic group is therefore also a topic
worthy of further attention. (See recent unpublished research findings
by David Cutler and Elizabeth Richardson (1997) and Angus Deaton
and Christina Paxson (1997).

References

Acs, Gregory, and John Sabelhaus. 1995. "Trends in Out-of-Pocket Spending on Health
Care, 1980–92." *Monthly Labor Review* 118(12):35–45.

---

37. For an early discussion of this issue in the Stigler Commission report, see Snyder
1961.

Amble, Nathan, and Ken Stewart. 1994. "Experimental Price Index for Elderly Consumers." *Monthly Labor Review* 117(5):11–6.

Armknecht, Paul A., Brent R. Moulton, and Kenneth J. Stewart. 1994. "Improvements to the Food at Home, Shelter and Prescription Drug Indexes in the U.S. Consumer Price Index." U.S. Department of Labor, Bureau of Labor Statistics, CPI Announcement-Version I, October 20.

Baker, Cathy, and Natalie Kramer. 1991. "Employer-Sponsored Prescription Drug Benefits." *Monthly Labor Review* 114(2):31–5.

Berndt, Ernst R., Iain Cockburn, and Zvi Griliches. 1996. "Pharmaceutical Innovations and Market Dynamics: Tracking Effects on Price Indexes for Antidepressant Drugs." In Martin N. Baily, Peter C. Reiss, and Clifford Winston, eds., *Brookings Papers on Economic Activity: Microeconomics 1996:* 133–88. Washington, D.C.: Brookings Institution.

Berndt, Ernst R., Zvi Griliches, and Joshua G. Rosett. 1993. "Auditing the Producer Price Index: Micro Evidence from Prescription Pharmaceutical Preparations." *Journal of Business and Economic Statistics* 11(3):251–64.

Caves, Richard E., Michael D. Whinston, and Mark A. Hurwitz. 1991. "Patent Expiration, Entry, and Competition in the U.S. Pharmaceutical Industry." In Martin Neil Baily and Clifford Winston, eds., *Brookings Papers on Economic Activity, Microeconomics, 1991,* 1–66. Washington, D.C.: Brookings Institution.

Cleeton, David L., Valy T. Goepfrich, and Burton A. Weisbrod. 1992. "What Does the Consumer Price Index for Prescription Drugs Really Measure?" *Health Care Financing Review* 13(3):45–51.

Cowan, Cathy A., Bradley R. Braden, Patricia A. McDonnell, and Lekha Sivarajan. 1996. "Business, Households, and Government: Health Spending, 1994." *Health Care Financing Review* 17(4):157–78.

Cutler, David M., Mark McClellan, Joseph P. Newhouse, and Dahlia Remler. 1996. "Are Medical Prices Declining?" Working Paper no. 5750, National Bureau of Economic Research, Cambridge, MA.

Cutler, David M., and Ellen Meara. 1997. "The Medical Cost of the Young and Old: A Forty Year Perspective. Paper presented at the National Bureau of Economic Research Conference on Aging, Boulder, CO, April 1997.

Cutler, David M., and Elizabeth Richardson. 1997. "Inequality in Health." Cambridge, MA: National Bureau of Economic Research. Unpublished.

Daugherty, James C. 1964. "Health Insurance in the Revised CPI." *Monthly Labor Review* 87(11):1299–300.

Deaton, Angus M., and Christina Paxson. 1997. "Health, Income and Inequality Over the Life Cycle." Princeton, NJ: Princeton University, Department of Economics. Unpublished.

Fixler, Dennis. 1996. "The Treatment of the Price of Health Insurance in the CPI." U.S. Department of Labor, Bureau of Labor Statistics, Washington, DC. Unpublished.

Ford, Ina Kay, and Philip Sturm. 1988. "CPI Revision Provides More Accuracy in the Medical Care Services Component." *Monthly Labor Review* 111(4):17–26.

Garner, Thesia I., David S. Johnson, and Mary F. Kokoski. 1996. "An Experimental Consumer Price Index for the Poor." *Monthly Labor Review* 119(9):32–42.

Gephardt, Richard A. 1997. "Budget Gimmick." *Washington Post*, 1 May, p. A23.

Getzen, Thomas E. 1992. "Medical Care Price Indexes: Theory, Construction and Empirical Analysis of the US Series, 1927–1990." In Richard M. Scheffler and Louis F. Rossiter, eds., *Advances in Health Economics and Health Services Research*, vol. 13: 83–128. Greenwich, CT: JAI Press.

Griliches, Zvi, and Iain Cockburn. 1994. "Generics and New Goods in Pharmaceutical Price Indexes." *American Economic Review* 84(5):1213–32.

Hitschler, Pamela B. 1993. "Spending by Older Consumers: 1980 and 1990 Compared." *Monthly Labor Review* 116(5):3–13.

IMS America. 1996. *Information Services Manual*. Plymouth Meeting, PA: IMS.

Kanoza, Douglas. 1996. "Supplemental Sampling in the PPI Pharmaceuticals Index." *Producer Price Indexes Detailed Price Report*, January, pp. 8–10.

Kuttner, Robert. 1997. "The CPI Fix." *Boston Globe*, March 10, p. A15.

Lane, Walter. 1996. "Changing the Item Structure of the Consumer Price Index." *Monthly Labor Review* 119(12):18–25.

Langford, Elizabeth. 1957. "Medical Care in the Consumer Price Index, 1935–56." *Monthly Labor Review* 80(9):1053–8.

Levit, Katharine R., Helen C. Lazenby, Bradley R. Braden, Cathy A. Cowan, Patricia A. McDonnell, Lekha Sivarajan, Jean M. Stiller, Darleen K. Won, Carolyn S. Donham, Anna M. Long, and Madie W. Stewart. 1996. "National Health Expenditures, 1995." *Health Care Financing Review* 18(1):175–214.

Lu, John, and William S. Comanor. 1996. "Strategic Pricing of New Pharmaceuticals." Working paper no. 96-1, UCLA School of Public Health, Research Program in Pharmaceutical Economics and Policy, Los Angeles, CA. (Forthcoming, *Review of Economics and Statistics*.)

Mason, Charles C. 1988. "An Analysis of the Rates of Inflation Affecting Older Americans Based on an Experimental Reweighted Consumer Price Index." Report presented to the U.S. Congress, June.

Masson, Alison, and Robert L. Steiner. 1985. *Generic Substitution and Prescription Prices: The Economic Effects of State Drug Laws*. Washington DC: Bureau of Economics, Federal Trade Commission.

Michael, Robert T. 1979. "Variation across Households in the Rate of Inflation." *Journal of Money, Credit and Banking* 11(1):32–44.

Moulton, Brent R., and Kenneth J. Stewart. 1997. "An Overview of Experimental U.S. Consumer Price Indexes." Washington, DC: U.S. Department of Labor, Bureau of Labor Statistics. Unpublished.

Pharmaceutical Research and Manufacturers of America. 1997. *1997 Industry Profile*. Washington, DC: Pharmaceutical Research and Manufacturers of America.

Rice, Dorothy P., and Loucele A. Horowitz. 1967. "Trends in Medical Care Prices." *Social Security Bulletin* 30(7):13–28.

Ristow, William. 1996. "IMS Presentation to the BLS." IMS America, Plymouth Meeting, PA, July. Mimeographed.

Rubin, Rose M., and Kenneth Koelin. 1996. "Elderly and Nonelderly Expenditures on Necessities in the 1980s." *Monthly Labor Review* 119(9):24–31.

Shapiro, Matthew D., and David W. Wilcox. 1996. "Mismeasurement in the Consumer Price Index: An Evaluation." Working paper no. 5590, National Bureau of Economic Research, Cambridge, MA. (Forthcoming, *NBER Macroeconomics Annual 1996*.)

Snyder, Eleanore M. 1961. "Cost of Living Indexes for Special Classes of Consumers." Staff Paper 7, in United States Congress, Committee on Joint Economic Activity, *Government Price Statistics*, Hearings before the Subcommittee on Economic Statistics of the Joint Economic Committee, Congress of the United States, 87th Congress, 1st Session, Pursuant to Sec. 5(a) of Public Law 304 (79th Congress), Part 1, January 24, 337–72.

Triplett, Jack E. 1997. "What's Different About Health? Human Repair and Car Repair in National Accounts." National Bureau of Economic Research, Cambridge, MA. Unpublished draft manuscript.

United States Department of Health, Education and Welfare. 1967. *Report to the President on Medical Care Prices.* Washington, DC: U.S. Government Printing Office.

United States Department of Labor, Bureau of Labor Statistics. Various years/issues. *CPI Detailed Report.* Washington, DC: U.S. Government Printing Office.

United States Department of Labor, Bureau of Labor Statistics. 1996. *Producer Price Indexes.* Washington, DC: U.S. Government Printing Office.

United States Department of Labor, Bureau of Labor Statistics. 1992. *Handbook of Methods.* Bulletin 2414. Washington, DC: U.S. Government Printing Office.

United States Senate Finance Committee. 1996. *Final Report from the Advisory Commission To Study The Consumer Price Index.* Washington DC: U.S. Government Printing Office.

3

Managed Care and the Growth of Medical Expenditures

David M. Cutler, *Harvard University and National Bureau of Economic Research*
Louise Sheiner, *Federal Reserve Board of Governors*

Executive Summary

We use data across states to examine the relation between HMO enrollment and medical spending. We find that increased managed care enrollment significantly reduces hospital cost growth. Although increased spending on physicians offsets some of this effect, we generally find a significant reduction in total spending as well. In analyzing the sources of hospital cost reductions, we find preliminary evidence that managed care has reduced the diffusion of medical technologies. States with high managed care enrollment were technology leaders in the early 1980s; by the early 1990s those states were only average in their acquisition of new technologies. This finding suggests managed care may significantly affect the long-run growth of medical spending.

Over the past few years, health insurance costs have made a dramatic turnaround. After decades of double-digit increases, health insurance cost growth has essentially ground to a halt. Most observers point to managed care as the leading culprit. "The growing dominance of managed care has helped control health care cost increases," the *New York Times* editorialized. "What this demonstrates is that in the private sector, managed care and competition are lowering the rate of cost increases in health care," Representative Nancy Johnson stated.

But the evidence on this point is far from compelling. Some surveys find that managed-care premiums are not much lower than traditional

David M. Cutler is Professor of Economics, Harvard University, and Research Associate, National Bureau of Economic Research. Louise Sheiner is an Economist at the Board of Governors of the Federal Reserve System. We are grateful to Anna Long at the Health Care Financing Administration for providing us with state medical spending data and Victor Fuchs for helpful comments. This research was supported by the National Institute on Aging and the Commonwealth Fund through grants to the NBER. This paper does not necessarily reflect the views of the members or staff of the Board of Governors of the Federal Reserve.

indemnity premiums (Krueger and Levy 1996), so the savings from enrollment shifts to managed care alone may not be that great. Further, managed-care enrollment in many parts of the country is still very low. Finally, the growth of public health programs has slowed as well— with both Medicare and Medicaid growing more slowly over the past few years than over the previous decade. Medicare has little managed-care enrollment, and although some have pointed to the growth of managed care as responsible for less-rapid cost growth in Medicaid, initial analysis indicates this was not the primary factor (Holahan and Liska 1997).[1]

And even if managed care is the answer, it is not clear whether this reduced rate of cost growth can continue. Continued excess capacity in the health system bodes well for future managed-care cost reductions. Hospital occupancy rates, for example, which were 78% in 1980, were 66% in 1995, even with a 12% reduction in hospital beds. In the presence of excess capacity, managed-care insurers find it easier to bargain among providers and achieve overall lower rates. But there is some concern that the increasing consolidation of the medical care sector may reduce the ability of managed-care insurers to bargain among providers.

More fundamentally, however, managed care may not be addressing the right problem. Managed-care insurers may lower the rates paid for particular services and may even chip away at the margins of medical care—for example, in reduced hospital stays. But the fundamental drivers of medical costs in the next several decades will be aging and medicine's expanding technological capability. The latter factor in particular has accounted for the bulk of the growth of medical costs historically, and it is not clear that managed care has done, or can do, much about this. Managed care may save money, but how much and for how long?

In this chapter, we examine whether managed care has affected the growth of medical costs, and if so, whether that effect will continue or slow down. We take advantage of the dramatic variation in the medical insurance environment across states. Managed care is the dominant (if not the only) source of medical insurance in some states; in California, for example, close to 80% of the population is enrolled in managed care. In other states, such as Alaska or Wyoming, managed care is

---

1. For example, growth in spending for the elderly and the blind (who are generally not enrolled in managed care) fell more than spending for children and adults.

virtually nonexistent. This variation in managed-care penetration provides a natural laboratory in which to examine the source of cost savings.

We conclude that managed care has slowed the growth of medical costs. States with high managed-care enrollment have significantly lower cost growth than states with lower managed-care enrollment. Managed care most affects hospital spending growth. Increased spending on physicians offsets some of the reduced hospital spending growth, but we typically find a net reduction in total spending growth. Perhaps more importantly, we find suggestive evidence that managed care may be reducing the diffusion of new medical technologies. States with high managed-care enrollment were technology "leaders" in the early 1980s but were only average in their use of technology in the early 1990s. This suggests that managed care may have a significant effect on the long-run growth of medical costs.

I. The Growth of Aggregate Medical Spending

We begin by analyzing recent changes in national health expenditures to examine whether there is any relation between increased competition and reduced medical spending growth. Figure 3.1 shows the growth of real, per capita national health expenditures for various time periods from 1960 through 1995. (Throughout the chapter, dollar amounts in real terms are adjusted using the GDP deflator for personal consumption expenditures.) Between 1960 and 1990, medical expenditures grew about 5% per year in real, per capita terms. The growth rate varied by decade. In the 1960s, growth was rapid, as Medicare and Medicaid were created and insurance coverage for the privately insured became more generous. In the 1970s, the medical sector consolidated and growth rates ebbed. The 1980s were marked by the first serious efforts at cost containment, including prospective payment for hospitals in the public sector and some of the private sector. But overall cost growth continued relatively unabated.

In the 1990s, however, and particularly since 1992, the growth of medical costs has slowed dramatically. In 1992, medical spending grew 4.8%. In 1993, growth was 3.1%; in 1994, it was 1.5%; and in 1995, it was 2.1%. This reduction in growth is particularly surprising given the ongoing economic expansion of the post-1992 period. (As we show below, the elasticity of medical spending with respect to income is about 1). Growth rates this low are thus extremely unusual historically.

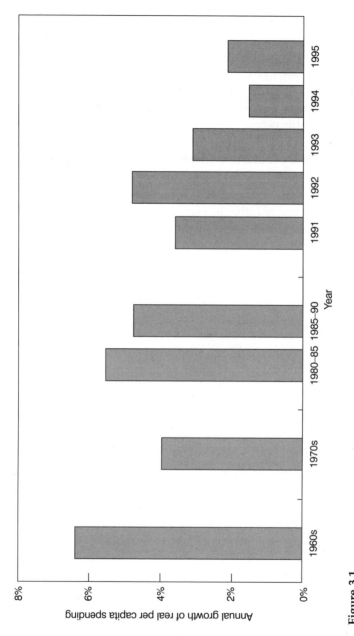

Figure 3.1
Growth rate of national health expenditures

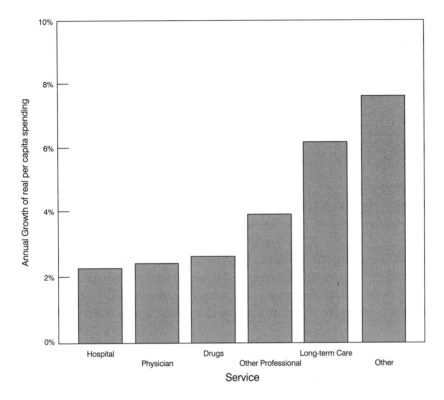

Figure 3.2
Growth of medical spending by service, 1990–1995

To offer more insight into why medical expenditure increases have been so low, figure 3.2 shows the growth in medical spending by service from 1990 to 1995. Acute-care spending (hospitals, physicians, and prescription drugs) has grown most slowly—each category about 2.5% per year. Together, these services account for about two-thirds of medical costs. Other professional services, long-term care services, and other spending have slowed by much less.

II. The Managed Care Explanation

A common depiction in newspapers and professional journals is that increased enrollment in managed care has resulted in the reduction in spending growth. The insurance environment has changed enormously over the past several years. In 1980, about 5% of the privately insured population was in managed care.[2] By 1987, managed care accounted for about one-quarter of the privately insured population (Gabel et al. 1987); today more than three-quarters of the privately insured population is enrolled in managed care (Jensen et al. 1997).

Of course, many types of health insurance plans fall under the rubric of "managed care." A fee-for-service plan with some utilization review, for example, may call itself a managed-care plan. Still, the change in plan enrollments has been impressive. Enrollment in the most restrictive form of managed care—health maintenance organizations [HMOs]—rose from 16% of insured workers in 1987 to 48% in 1995 (including point-of-service plans).[3] Enrollment in preferred provider organizations [PPOs], the next-most-restrictive form of managed care, rose from 11% in 1987 to 25% in 1995.

Managed care can reduce medical cost growth through three mechanisms. First, managed care might negotiate price reductions. Because much of a physician's earnings are a return on past investment, managed care can often induce physicians to accept lower fees than they would otherwise have charged. The same is true for prescription drugs, some hospital services, and some medical durables. These discounts reduce medical costs.[4] These will be one-time savings: As prices fall, medical spending growth will slow, but after the return to past investment has been squeezed out, medical costs will resume their increase.

Managed care might also save money through one-time quantity reductions. For example, managed-care insurers monitor very carefully the number of days that their enrollees are in the hospital. If stays can be reduced by a day, costs fall.[5] Again, however, these are likely

---

2. Even with the managed care available, there was little competition with indemnity insurers. Employers often subsidized indemnity policies heavily, blunting the incentives for HMOs to limit spending.

3. The distinction between HMOs and other forms of managed care has become less clear over time. In general, however, HMOs require participants to receive care from particular providers and typically pay primary-care physicians on a salary or capitated basis. Preferred provider organizations pay their providers on a discounted fee-for-service basis but may also monitor physician behavior to exclude physicians who do not keep utilization down. In both types of plans, cost sharing to the insured for using a provider in the insurer's network is lower than for using providers outside the network.

4. These price reductions may have long-term effects on the supply of new physicians or medical equipment, but we ignore that issue in this chapter.

5. Again, this change may have long-term effects on the number of hospitals, the structure of the hospital industry, and the like, but for our purposes, we ignore these effects.

to be one-time savings. Lengths of stay can fall only so much; when they cease falling, medical costs will continue to increase.

Finally, managed care might save money by reducing the rate of technology expansion—the intensity with which a typical patient is treated or the rate at which new technologies are adopted. We separate this factor from the first two because of its importance in the long-run growth of medical spending. Much research shows that the dominant source of increasing medical costs over time is the development of new medical technologies and the application of existing technologies to new patients (Aaron 1991; Newhouse 1992; Cutler and McClellan 1996). If managed care reduces the expansion of technologies, it could have a long-term effect on the growth of medical costs.

Quantity changes resulting from managed care—either one-time savings or reductions in the rate of technology diffusion—may either improve or reduce welfare. To the extent that managed care reduces the resources needed to provide a given level of medical services, that would be an efficiency savings to society. If managed care changes the amount of services provided, however, welfare may either rise or fall, depending on whether the services no longer provided were worth more or less than their cost. In this chapter, we look only at the effects of managed care on overall resource utilization, without drawing strong conclusions about the value of those changes.

Testing the Managed-Care Effect

One piece of evidence suggesting that managed care has reduced national medical expenditures in the past few years is that managed-care premiums are lower than premiums in traditional indemnity policies. A recent Foster Higgins report, for example, found that in 1995, costs for HMOs were either flat or declining, whereas costs for traditional insurance continued to rise. Hay-Huggins reports that HMO premiums are significantly lower than premiums for fee-for-service insurance, although other surveys show smaller differences (Krueger and Levy 1997). Wholey, Feldman, and Christianson (1995) examine the impact of HMO concentration on changes in HMO premiums and find that more HMO competition leads to lower HMO premiums.

But this evidence is not conclusive. The fact that managed care pays less than indemnity insurers does not mean that total medical spending is lower. Providers might simply reduce their costs to managed-care insurers and raise them to indemnity insurers to offset the managed-care discount. This type of substitution is broadly believed to occur when Medicare and Medicaid cut spending. Or managed care might reduce spending for covered services, but spending for uncovered services might rise. On the other hand, if competition induces changes in practice styles so that HMOs have a moderating effect on both HMO and traditional indemnity premiums,[6] then comparing HMO to fee-for-service premiums may understate managed care's impact on health expenditures.

We estimate the systemwide savings from managed care by looking at overall medical spending growth in states where managed care is more prevalent compared to states where managed care is less prevalent. If managed care reduces medical spending growth, this should be apparent through such a comparison.

Figure 3.3 shows a first pass at this comparison. We show per capita spending relative to the national average in California and Minnesota—two states in the vanguard of the managed-care revolution—between 1980 and 1993. In both states, spending growth was much lower than the national average. In California, for example, per capita medical spending was 17% above the national average in 1980; by 1993 spending was equal to the national average. In Minnesota, medical spending fell from 9% above the national average to 4% above the national average over the same period.

Melnick and Zwanziger (1995) and Zwanziger and Melnick (1996) compare in detail the experience of California with that of the rest of the nation. They show that in the 1980s, spending on all acute-care services rose less rapidly in California than in the nation as a whole, as did numbers of full-time-equivalent hospital employees per patient and the average length of a hospital stay.

To examine this issue more systematically, we use data on state medical spending between 1980 and 1993 from the Health Care Financing Administration. (See Levit et al. (1995) for a description of the data.) Unfortunately, no more recent data on cross-state spending are available; thus, we cannot examine managed care's effects in the period in which the national changes in spending were the greatest. We

---

6. For example, Wickizer and Feldstein (1995) found that premiums for fee-for-service insurance were lower in areas with higher HMO enrollment. Baker (1997) found that Medicare fee-for-service payments were lower in areas with more managed care.

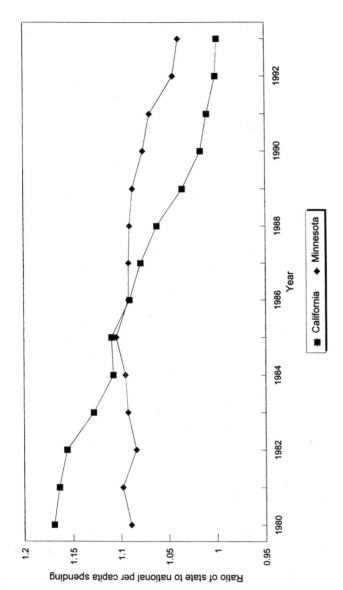

Figure 3.3
Relative medical spending in California and Minnesota (state per capita spending/ national average per capita spending)

measure HMO enrollment as the average value, from 1980 to 1993, of HMO enrollment per capita (HMO enrollment data are from Interstudy).

Table 3.1 shows summary statistics for the data. The average state had spending growth of 4.6% in real per capita terms between 1980 and 1993, with hospital spending growing less rapidly than physician spending. HMO enrollment averaged 11.2%, but ranged from 0% to 28%. (HMO enrollment includes both "pure" enrollment (closed-panel HMOs) and "open" enrollment (plans with a point-of-service option)). Although there are many other forms of managed care beyond HMOs, consistent data on non-HMO managed care are not available over time. We also suspect that HMO enrollment is correlated with managed-care enrollment more generally. The states with the highest HMO enrollments are California, Minnesota, Hawaii, Oregon, and Massachusetts. Those with the lowest HMO enrollments are small or rural states such as Alaska, Mississippi, and Wyoming, with no HMO enrollment or a very small amount.

Figure 3.4 shows the national analog of figure 3.3. We graph the change in real per capita medical expenditures for each state against average HMO enrollment. The two have a clear negative relation, consistent with the managed-care explanation. States with high HMO enrollment had less-rapid spending growth. The correlation between cost growth and HMO enrollment, shown in the bottom of table 3.1, is −.6. And a simple regression equation gives a large magnitude: Each ten-percentage-point increase in HMO enrollment reduces cost growth by .6 percentage points annually.[7]

Before being convinced by figure 3.4, however, we must question why managed-care enrollment is so high in some states and so low in others. Both managed-care enrollment and subsequent spending growth may respond to a third factor—the initial level of medical spending in the state. In states where costs are high, managed care will enroll new members more easily than in states where they are low. But this relationship is problematic if states with high medical costs naturally would have had less-rapid growth of medical costs in the future, perhaps because other states would catch up to their more advanced

---

7. All of our correlations and regressions weight the observations by population. Without such weighting, HMOs would not have as large or significant an effect on expenditures (both because states like Alaska, Nevada, and Hawaii are outliers but have very small populations and because weighting the regressions places more weight on California).

Table 3.1
Summary statistics for state data, 1980–1993

Statistic	Average HMO enrollment	ΔMedical spending	ΔHospital spending	ΔPhysician spending	ΔPersonal income	Initial medical spending
Mean	11.2%	4.6%	3.7%	4.9%	1.4%	$1,666
Standard deviation	7.7	0.8	1.1	.9	0.6	228
Minimum	0.0	2.4	1.2	1.4	-.30	1,160
Maximum	27.6	6.4	5.9	8.0	2.2	2,030
Correlations						
Average HMO enrollment	1.00					
ΔMedical spending	-.62	1.00				
ΔHospital spending	-.73	.89	1.00			
ΔPhysician spending	-.04	.66	.34	1.00		
ΔPersonal income	-.42	.72	.52	.67	1.00	
Initial medical spending	.73	-.53	-.69	-.01	-.19	1.00

Note: Data are for 50 states (excluding the District of Columbia). All changes are from 1980 to 1993. Initial medical spending is in 1980. Medical spending and income are in real, per capita terms and growth rates are annualized. HMO enrollment is the average between 1980 and 1993. Statistics are weighted by population in 1993.

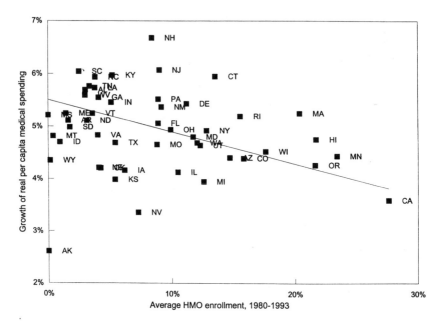

Figure 3.4
HMO enrollment and the growth of medical spending, 1980–1993

medical practices. Indeed, as figure 3.3 showed, medical expenditures in California slowed just enough to bring California spending back to the national average from the extremely high levels observed in the early 1980s.

Figures 3.5 and 3.6 suggest this is a more general phenomenon. Figure 3.5 shows the relation between per capita medical spending in 1980 and average HMO enrollment between 1980 and 1993. Initial spending and managed-care enrollment are positively related; the correlation between them, shown in table 3.1, is .73. Figure 3.6 shows that initial medical spending is also associated with reductions in the growth of future medical spending. Again, the correlation is large (−.53).

The important question, then, is whether managed-care enrollment really reduces the growth rate of medical spending or whether it instead proxies for states with high initial spending, which naturally have less rapid growth rates over time. In the next section, we address this issue.

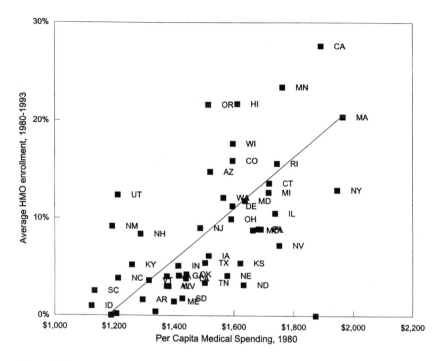

Figure 3.5
Initial medical spending and average subsequent HMO enrollment

III. Explaining State Cost Growth

To estimate the effect of managed care on the growth of state medical costs, we consider the regression analogue to figure 3.4:

$$\Delta Spending_s = \beta_1\ HMO\ Enrollment_s + X_s\beta + \varepsilon_s, \tag{3.1}$$

where s denotes states and the dependent variable is the annualized growth rate of real, per capita medical spending in the state from 1980 to 1993. β_1 is the effect of HMO enrollment on annual cost growth.

We examine managed care's impact on a number of components of spending—total medical spending, spending on hospitals, spending on physicians, and spending on prescription drugs. We also examine its impact separately on Medicare and non-Medicare expenditures. Ideally, we would like to measure managed care's impact on the per capita spending of privately insured individuals, but those data are not available. Non-Medicare expenditures are a decent proxy, but in addition to the health expenditures of privately insured individuals, non-Medicare expenditures include out-of-pocket expenditures of the

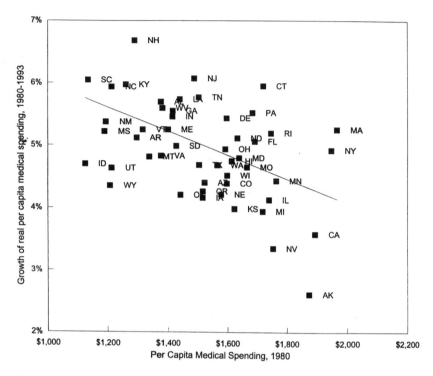

Figure 3.6
Reversion of medical spending

elderly and the uninsured and expenditures paid by Medicaid or other
government programs.

It is not clear whether the level or the change in HMO enrollment
should be related to the growth of spending. In theory, the level of
managed care could affect both the level of spending, through one-
time efficiency gains or reimbursement cuts (so the change in HMO
enrollment would be related to the change in spending), or the growth
rate of spending, by changing the speed at which technology is
adopted (so the level of HMO enrollment would explain changes in
spending). In practice, however, the one-time effects of high HMO
enrollment likely occur over a number of years, so that the level of
managed-care enrollment in a state is likely to affect the growth rate of
spending regardless of whether HMOs affect technology adoption.
Further, the change in HMO enrollment might affect spending only
with a lag. For these reasons, we have decided to use the average level
of HMO enrollment over the period in our regressions. As figure 3.7

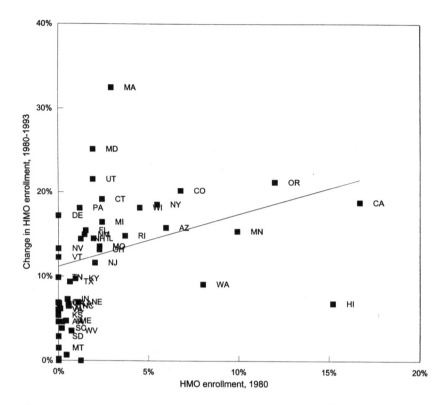

Figure 3.7
Level and growth of HMO enrollment

shows, however, the change in HMO enrollment is closely correlated with the level of HMO enrollment in 1980; in general, our results hold equally well when we use the change in HMO enrollment instead of the level.[8]

The other right-hand-side variables included in the regression are the change in per capita income, because people with higher incomes spend more on health care (Newhouse and the Insurance Experiment Group 1993), and demographic controls (the change in fraction of the population 18 or younger and the change in fraction of the population 65 or older).

---

8. The level of HMO enrollment has a sufficiently high correlation with its growth rate that the standard errors increase substantially when we include both in the regression simultaneously.

Table 3.2 presents regression results for total health spending over 1980–93. The first four columns show figures without controlling for initial spending; the second four columns include such controls. In general, the coefficients on the control variables are as we would expect. Income growth is positively related to spending growth; the elasticity is about 1. An increasing share of older people is associated with increased medical spending, whereas an increasing share of younger people has no effect on spending growth.

The first row shows the effect of HMO enrollment on cost growth. When initial spending levels are not controlled, HMOs have a significant negative effect on total health spending. Every ten-percentage-point increase in HMO enrollment reduces the growth of health expenditures by 3 percentage points per year.[9] The effect works only through hospital spending—increased HMO enrollment is actually associated with increased spending on physicians and prescription drugs.

Consistent with our figures above, controlling for initial spending reduces HMOs' impact on cost growth. Initial spending has a strong negative effect on subsequent spending growth; each 10% increase in spending in 1980 is associated with cost growth between 1980 and 1993 that is .2 percentage points below average. Whatever the source of this convergence, it is not a new phenomenon. As reported in table 3.3, growth of medical expenditures across states exhibited the same pattern from 1966 to 1980. Controlling for this phenomenon is important and affects our estimates of managed care's impact on health costs. Returning to table 3.2, when we control for initial spending, the coefficient of HMO enrollment on total spending is still negative (−.014) but not statistically significant. Even in this case, however, HMOs are still associated with a reduction in hospital spending; the coefficient is large (−.052) and statistically significant. But HMOs also have a positive, large, statistically significant impact on physician spending.

Clearly, one of managed care's major effects is to shift the site of care from the hospital to the physician's office or clinic (see Reinhardt 1996 for a discussion of this trend). As shown in figure 3.8, states with high HMO enrollments spend much less of their medical dollars in the

---

9. An alternative way to see this effect is to regress the logarithm of medical spending in each year on HMO enrollment that year and the control variables for that year. If we do this, we obtain a coefficient on HMO enrollment of .688 (.214) in 1980 and .198 (.125) in 1993. The reduction in the coefficient on HMO enrollment is consistent with the regressions in table 3.2.

Table 3.2
Managed care and total spending growth, 1980–1993

Independent variable	Without initial spending				With initial spending			
	Total	Component of spending			Total	Component of spending		
		Hospital	Physician	Drug		Hospital	Physician	Drug
HMO enrollment	-.034	-.080	.042	.030	-.014	-.052	.072	.019
	(.011)	(.017)	(.016)	(.014)	(.013)	(.015)	(.017)	(.013)
ΔPersonal income	.772	.501	1.341	.974	.897	.764	1.448	.784
	(.147)	(.221)	(.212)	(.193)	(.144)	(.194)	(1.401)	(.179)
ΔPercentage of population younger than 19	.370	.764	.282	.371	1.300	1.863	1.844	-.278
	(.991)	(1.488)	(1.428)	(1.353)	(.984)	(1.271)	(1.376)	(1.170)
ΔPercentage of population older than 64	2.803	2.893	2.735	4.619	2.781	3.503	1.448	3.859
	(1.032)	(1.549)	(1.428)	(1.353)	(.963)	(1.306)	(1.401)	(1.222)
ln(initial medical spending)	—	—	—	—	-.019	-.026	-.027	-.029
					(.007)	(.006)	(.008)	(.008)
Summary statistics								
N	50	50	50	50	50	50	50	50
R^2	.664	.578	.518	.476	.707	.703	.605	.586

Note: Data are for 50 states (excluding the District of Columbia). All changes are from 1980 to 1993. Initial medical spending is in 1980. Medical spending and income are in real, per capita terms and growth rates are annualized. HMO enrollment is the average between 1980 to 1993. Regressions are weighted by state population in 1993.

Table 3.3
Reversion of spending, 1966–1980

Independent variable	Component of spending			
	Total	Hospital	Physician	Drug
HMO enrollment	—	—	—	—
ΔPersonal income	.213	−.161	1.173	.575
	(.163)	(.208)	(.279)	(.173)
ΔPercentage of population younger than 19	−.036	.122	−.482	.035
	(.074)	(.097)	(.129)	(.092)
ΔPercentage of population older than 64	.309	.400	.164	.143
	(.087)	(.113)	(.148)	(.106)
ln(initial medical spending)	−.018	−.021	−.006	−.042
	(.005)	(.005)	(.007)	(.007)
Summary statistics				
N	50	50	50	50
R^2	.589	.466	.634	.623

Note: Data are for 50 states (excluding the District of Columbia). All changes are from 1966 to 1980. Initial medical spending is in 1966. Medical spending and income are in real, per capita terms and growth rates are annualized. Regressions are weighted by state population in 1980.

hospital. HMO coverage does not affect the share of spending on drugs; most of the offset is on physicians. HMOs' large impact on physician spending is somewhat surprising and is worthy of further investigation.[10]

Table 3.4 shows regression analogous to those in table 3.2 for non-Medicare expenditures. The results are very similar—when we do not control for initial spending, HMOs reduce total and hospital spending but increase physician and prescription drug spending. When initial spending is included, HMOs have no significant effect on total health spending but shift spending from hospitals to physicians.

Table 3.5 examines managed care's effect on Medicare expenditures per elderly person. (Because Medicare does not pay for prescription drug coverage, only the physician and hospital results are presented.) Controlling for initial spending, the results indicate that states with high HMO enrollment (mostly of the non-Medicare population) have

---

10. Simon and Emmons (1997) find that physicians who are paid through capitation often do not purchase reinsurance. It is possible, then, that payments to physicians increase under managed care because physicians take on increased risk. Alternatively, some physician spending could actually be hospital spending, but under systems of capitated payments, the two may be hard to distinguish.

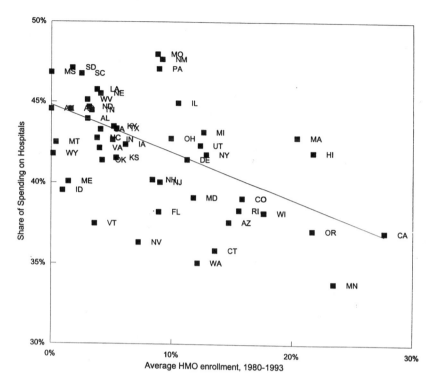

Figure 3.8
Managed care and the share of spending on hospitals

lower hospital spending growth, although the coefficient is not significant at a 10% level. HMOs have no measured effect on physicians.
Because enrollment in managed care was a very small share of total
Medicare enrollment in this time period, the effect of managed care on
Medicare costs is not a direct effect of managed care enrollment for that
group. Instead, two effects might be at work. First, to the extent that
managed care affects hospital or physician practices, states with a high
rate of HMO enrollment might also have lower Medicare expenditures.
Second, HMOs may reduce the amount of "cost-shifting" from Medicare to private insurance, which would show up as lower overall
spending and probably fewer services to the Medicare population.
Further work could usefully distinguish between these effects.

Our analysis to this point raises two issues. First, the health care
market has changed significantly in recent years (although some may
argue that most of the changes have occurred in the years since 1993,
for which expenditure data across states are not yet available), and

Table 3.4
Managed care and private spending growth, 1980–1993

Independent variable	Without initial spending			With initial spending		
		Component of spending			Component of spending	
	Total	Hospital	Physician	Total	Hospital	Physician
HMO enrollment	-.025	-.078	.056	-.008	-.050	.095
	(.010)	(.018)	(.018)	(.012)	(.016)	(.019)
ΔPersonal income	.836	.476	1.589	.938	.767	1.100
	(.134)	(.234)	(.239)	(.134)	(.208)	(.247)
ΔPercentage of population younger than 19	.283	.734	.149	.961	1.638	1.165
	(.905)	(1.582)	(1.612)	(.903)	(1.344)	(1.441)
ΔPercentage of population older than 64	3.439	3.538	1.864	3.324	3.836	.174
	(.942)	(1.647)	(1.678)	(.896)	(1.386)	(1.540)
ln(initial medical spending)	—	—	—	-.015	-.027	-.034
				(.006)	(.006)	(.009)
Summary statistics						
N	50	50	50	50	50	50
R^2	.714	.552	.530	.742	.684	.637

Note: Data are for 50 states (excluding the District of Columbia). All changes are from 1980 to 1993. Initial medical spending is in 1980. Medical spending and income are in real, per capita terms and growth rates are annualized. HMO enrollment is the average between 1980 and 1993. Regressions are weighted by state population in 1993.

Table 3.5
Managed care and Medicare spending growth, 1980–1993

	Without initial spending			With initial spending		
	Total	Component of spending		Total	Component of spending	
Independent variable		Hospital	Physician		Hospital	Physician
HMO enrollment	-.072	-.083	-.010	-.036	-.037	-.001
	(.021)	(.023)	(.018)	(.024)	(.023)	(.020)
ΔPersonal income	.471	.662	-.007	.520	.596	.085
	(.286)	(.304)	(.239)	(.268)	(.262)	(.248)
ΔPercentage of population younger than 19	.741	1.224	-1.234	1.953	1.509	-.070
	(1.925)	(2.050)	(1.613)	(1.853)	(1.762)	(1.842)
ΔPercentage of population older than 64	-3.126	-3.922	3.138	-2.527	-2.265	1.687
	(2.005)	(2.134)	(1.679)	(1.886)	(1.877)	(1.705)
ln(initial medical spending)	—	—	—	-.028	-.036	-.008
				(.010)	(.009)	(.006)
Summary statistics						
N	50	50	50	50	50	50
R^2	.294	.347	.108	.383	.518	.121

Note: Data are for 50 states (excluding the District of Columbia). All changes are from 1980 to 1993. Initial medical spending is in 1980. Medical spending and income are in real, per capita terms and growth rates are annualized. HMO enrollment is the average between 1980 and 1993. Regressions are weighted by state population in 1993.

HMOs may have had increasing effects over time.[11] Second, these regressions ignore another major innovation in hospital financing that occurred in the 1980s—the introduction of prospective payment in Medicare. To the extent that prospective payment equalized payments across states (moving from a payment method that relied on reasonable costs to one of fixed payments per diagnosis), this would affect hospital spending as well. Because high-HMO states were also high-cost states, this may be negatively correlated with HMO enrollment.

To control for both of these issues, we reestimate the regressions for 1988–93 only. By 1988, prospective payment was fully phased in and managed care was well underway. Thus, this time period might be more indicative of a true managed-care effect than 1983–88. Tables 3.6–3.8 present the results. The results for total spending growth, shown in table 3.6, indicate that managed care is more effective at controlling costs in the later period than in the earlier period; there is a greater negative effect on hospital spending growth and a smaller positive effect on physician spending growth.[12] The overall effect is a decline of .5 percentage points per year in total health expenditures for every ten-percentage-point increase in the HMO enrollment rate, a large effect and significantly different from zero. Table 3.7 shows similar results for private spending growth, although the positive effect of managed care on physician spending is larger and more significant. Table 3.8 shows that the results for Medicare growth again suggest a managed-care effect, but the coefficients are smaller and less significant over 1988–93 than over the entire 1980–93 period. This might indicate some confounding effects from the introduction of the Medicare Prospective Payment System (PPS) in the first part of the sample.

Overall, the cross-state evidence points to managed care as an important factor in the recent decline in health costs. Over the entire period from 1980 to 1993, we find that increases in physician spending nearly fully offset reductions in hospital spending. When we look at the most recent period, however, we find reductions in hospital spending only partly offset by increased physician spending. Our results suggest that a 10% increase in HMO enrollment reduces the growth of hospital spending by about 0.5% and that of overall medical costs

---

11. Gabel (1997) surveys the changes in HMOs that occurred in the 1990s.
12. Simon and Born (1996) find that managed care had no significant impact on physician earnings until 1993–94.

Table 3.6
Managed care and total spending growth, 1988–1993

Independent variable	Without initial spending				With initial spending			
		Component of spending				Component of spending		
	Total	Hospital	Physician	Drug	Total	Hospital	Physician	Drug
HMO enrollment	-.050	-.058	-.010	-.010	-.050	-.058	.035	-.005
	(.018)	(.025)	(.032)	(.014)	(.019)	(.025)	(.029)	(.021)
ΔPersonal income	.294	.664	-.327	.069	.295	.651	-.554	-.278
	(.199)	(.277)	(.354)	(.215)	(.201)	(.282)	(.302)	(.212)
ΔPercentage of population younger than 19	.717	.958	1.403	2.178	.690	1.011	3.820	1.156
	(.921)	(1.284)	(1.640)	(.997)	(.987)	(1.306)	(1.486)	(.873)
ΔPercentage of population older than 64	3.210	4.140	1.186	-.480	3.191	4.386	-1.113	1.791
	(1.331)	(1.855)	(2.368)	(1.441)	(1.364)	(2.006)	(2.062)	(1.388)
ln(initial medical spending)	—	—	—	—	.0009	-.004	-.060	-.038
					(.010)	(.012)	(.014)	(.010)
Summary statistics								
N	50	50	50	50	50	50	50	50
R^2	.492	.521	.009	.046	.480	.511	.297	.269

Note: Data are for 50 states (excluding the District of Columbia). All changes are from 1980 to 1993. Initial medical spending is in 1980. Medical spending and income are in real, per capita terms and growth rates are annualized. HMO enrollment is the average between 1980 and 1993. Regressions are weighted by state population in 1993.

Table 3.7
Managed care and private spending growth, 1988–1993

Independent variable	Without initial spending			With initial spending		
	Total	Component of spending		Total	Component of spending	
		Hospital	Physician		Hospital	Physician
HMO enrollment	-.040	-.055	-.002	-.039	-.051	.069
	(.019)	(.032)	(.038)	(.021)	(.032)	(.037)
ΔPersonal income	.432	.917	-.248	.430	.842	-.515
	(.217)	(.356)	(.428)	(.220)	(.356)	(.374)
ΔPercentage of population younger than 19	.752	1.529	.861	.825	1.577	2.496
	(1.007)	(1.649)	(1.984)	(1.060)	(1.638)	(1.754)
ΔPercentage of population older than 64	3.649	4.026	2.135	3.703	5.141	-.938
	(1.455)	(2.381)	(2.865)	(1.486)	(2.524)	(2.578)
ln(initial medical spending)	—	—	—	-.003	-.017	-.068
				(.011)	(.014)	(.016)
Summary statistics						
N	50	50	50	50	50	50
R^2	.466	.435	-.029	.454	.442	.238

Note: Data are for 50 states (excluding the District of Columbia). All changes are from 1980 to 1993. Initial medical spending is in 1980. Medical spending and income are in real, per capita terms and growth rates are annualized. HMO enrollment is the average between 1980 and 1993. Regressions are weighted by state population in 1993.

Table 3.8
Managed care and Medicare spending growth, 1988–1993

Independent variable	Without initial spending			With initial spending		
	Total	Component of spending		Total	Component of spending	
		Hospital	Physician		Hospital	Physician
HMO enrollment	-.068	-.058	-.029	-.071	-.065	-.024
	(.029)	(.029)	(.037)	(.029)	(.030)	(.035)
ΔPersonal income	-.311	-.028	-.384	-.270	.011	-.578
	(.323)	(.324)	(.409)	(.331)	(.326)	(.395)
ΔPercentage of population younger than 19	-.694	-1.084	2.994	-.969	-1.234	4.980
	(1.497)	(1.649)	(1.898)	(1.567)	(1.507)	(1.966)
ΔPercentage of population older than 64	-.454	.549	-3.099	-.602	-.020	-3.802
	(2.162)	(2.167)	(2.741)	(2.189)	(2.235)	(2.611)
ln(initial medical spending)	—	—	—	.010	.016	-.030
				(.016)	(.016)	(.012)
Summary statistics						
N	50	50	50	50	50	50
R^2	.134	.205	.076	.122	.206	.172

Note: Data are for 50 states (excluding the District of Columbia). All changes are from 1980 to 1993. Initial medical spending is in 1980. Medical spending and income are in real, per capita terms and growth rates are annualized. HMO enrollment is the average between 1980 and 1993. Regressions are weighted by state population in 1993.

by about 0.4%. These results are generally robust to a number of controls, including income, demographics, and the initial level of state spending.

IV. Explaining the Reduction in Hospital Costs

To predict the longer-run effects of managed care, it is important to know not only whether managed care has affected medical spending, but how it has done so. Has managed care simply extracted rents from providers—reducing payments for procedures or cutting back at the margins? Or has there been a more significant change in the medical environment. In this section, we examine changes in hospital costs to address this issue.

We start with an accounting identity. Per capita spending on hospital care is the product of spending per day in the hospital times the average length of stay per admission times the number of hospital admissions per capita:

$$
\left(\frac{Spending}{Capita}\right) = \left(\frac{Spending}{Admissions}\right) \cdot \left(\frac{Admissions}{Capita}\right)
$$

$$
= \left(\frac{Spending}{Days}\right) \cdot \left(\frac{Days}{Admissions}\right) \cdot \left(\frac{Admissions}{Capita}\right). \tag{3.2}
$$

The growth of medical spending per capita can therefore be decomposed into the growth of each of these terms.

The first rows of table 3.9 show regression equations for the growth of hospital spending per adjusted admission and adjusted admissions per capita.[13] Adjusted admissions are hospital admissions plus a factor to account for outpatient services provided, so that this figure approximates the total amount of hospital care provided. As the first row shows, HMOs have no significant effect on adjusted admissions per capita. The implication, shown in the second row, is that the entire decline in hospital growth associated with HMOs comes from a reduction in costs per admission. Decomposing this factor into days of care and costs per day (the next four rows) reveals that most of the reduction in the costs per admission comes from a reduction in the length of hospital stays. On average, a ten-percentage-point increase in the frac-

13. The coefficients shown in the table are those on the average HMO enrollment and those on the initial hospital spending, but the regressions also include the change in per capita income and the change in the population shares of old and young.

Table 3.9
HMO enrollment and components of hospital spending

Change in	1980–1993		1988–1993	
	Average HMO enrollment	Initial hospital spending	Average HMO enrollment	Initial hospital spending
Adjusted admissions per person	.018	.011	.019	.014
	(.013)	(.004)	(.017)	(.006)
Cost per adjusted admission	−.065	−.030	−.093	−.017
	(.016)	(.005)	(.034)	(.013)
Length of stay per admission				
All	−.053	−.006	−.080	.006
	(.021)	(.007)	(.025)	(.009)
Private	−.716	−.084	−.417	.035
	(.378)	(.125)	(.178)	(.067)
Medicare	−.551	−.123	−.283	−.012
	(.221)	(.073)	(.156)	(.058)
Costs per inpatient day	−.013	−.023	−.013	−.021
	(.022)	(.007)	(.027)	(.010)
Adjusted days per person	−.033	.003	−.061	.018
	(.022)	(.007)	(.025)	(.009)
Outpatient visits per person	−.053	.029	.026	.077
	(.038)	(.012)	(.058)	(.022)
Full-time hospital employees per person	−.060	−.006	−.056	−.006
	(.018)	(.006)	(.025)	(.010)
Hospital beds per person	−.045	.003	−.076	.019
	(.017)	(.006)	(.028)	(.010)

Note: All regressions include change in real per capita income and changes in fraction of population younger than 20 and older than 64. Data are for 50 states and are weighted by 1993 population.

tion of the population enrolled in HMOs leads to lengths of stay declining 0.5 percentage points faster per year. HMOs have a negative but insignificant effect on the average cost per day in the hospital.

The finding that all of the cost savings are in shorter hospital stays may be somewhat misleading. Because the amount of care given to a patient likely declines with additional days in the hospital, one might have expected states that experienced a greater reduction in length of stay to have shown an increase in the average cost per day. When controlling for length of stay, HMO enrollment does reduce cost per day.[14]

Direct measures of hospital resource utilization also vary with managed care. On average, states with a large fraction of their populations enrolled in HMOs have slower growth of hospital employees per person and less bed growth per person.

The table's right columns show the results for 1988–93. HMOs have a slightly larger effect on costs per admission in this period relative to the whole time period, consistent with our earlier results. Also, total days in the hospital (including an adjustment for outpatient visits) have declined significantly more in states with high HMO enrollment, although again HMOs have not significantly affected the costs per inpatient day. Length of stay for Medicare beneficiaries in this post-PPS adjustment period have also declined in states with high HMO enrollment, again indicating that changes in hospital practice styles have spillover effects.

V. Changes in Technology Adoption

We are particularly interested in the extent to which managed care has reduced the diffusion of medical technology, because that directly measures its long-run impact on cost growth. We thus examine this issue in some detail, using data on the adoption of specific technologies across states from the American Hospital Association's [AHA] annual survey, which asks whether hospitals have acquired a variety of important and expensive technologies. We analyze survey responses for

---

14. When the change in the length of stay is included in the regression, the effect of a ten-percentage-point increase in HMO enrollment is to reduce the growth of costs per day by 0.5 percentage points per year. Over 1988–93, however, the effect of HMO enrollment on costs per day is only about half this magnitude and is statistically insignificant.

1980, 1985, 1990, and 1995 to look at how managed-care enrollment affects technology diffusion over time.[15]

Our ideal measure of technology diffusion is the rate at which particular technologies are used for patients with similar clinical conditions. The AHA does not ask about technology use, however, only whether the hospital owns the technology. We thus use as our measure of technology diffusion the number of units of each technology per million persons in the state.[16] If all units perform roughly the same number of procedures, this accurately measures technology diffusion. If managed care consolidates technologies into some hospitals and keeps it out of other hospitals, however, we might find that managed care reduces technology's availability when in fact it does not reduce its actual utilization. Unfortunately, there is no way to surmount this issue without detailed information that we do not have on the use of particular procedures.

Table 3.10 shows the range of technologies we analyze, which are in five groups: cardiac technologies (catheterization lab, open-heart surgery facilities, and angioplasty facilities); radiation therapy (megavoltage radiation, radioactive implants, therapeutic radioisotope, X-ray therapies, and stereotactic radiosurgery); diagnostic radiology (CT scanner, diagnostic radioisotope, MRI, ultrasound, positron emission tomography [PET], and single photon emission computed tomography [SPECT]); transplantation services (kidney, organ [other than kidney], tissue, bone marrow); and other (extracorporeal shock wave lithotripter).

Perhaps more important than their grouping by service, however, our data are a mix of diffusing technologies and technologies that have already diffused. Catheterization labs, for example, go from four per million in 1980 to seven per million by 1995; CT scanners go from five per million in 1980 to twenty per million in 1995. Other technologies, such as radioactive implants and ultrasound machines, had already diffused by this time period. We classify the technologies that are diffusing over our time period into one group (the diffusing sample):

---

15. If a hospital does not respond to the AHA survey in some year, it has missing data about technologies. We use data on the previous four years of responses to impute technology ownership, where possible.

16. An alternative measure of technology availability would be the share of hospitals with a particular technology. This would be particularly sensitive to changes in the number of hospitals, however, which our earlier results suggest managed care affects. We thus do not use this measure.

Table 3.10
Diffusion of medical technologies

Technology	Units per million people			
	1980	1985	1990	1995
Cardiac				
Catheterization	4.1	4.6	6.2	6.8
Open-heart surgery	2.7	3.0	3.7	4.0
Angioplasty	—	—	4.6	4.7
Radiation therapy	—	—	—	5.0
Megavoltage radiation	3.8	4.1	4.2	—
Radioactive implants	5.9	5.9	5.1	—
Therapeutic radioisotope	6.8	6.1	5.6	—
X-ray therapy	5.5	4.4	4.0	—
Stereotactic radiosurgery	—	—	1.1	—
Diagnostic radiology				
CT scanner	5.2	13.3	17.7	19.7
Diagnostic radioisotope	18.7	17.0	16.0	14.0
MRI	—	1.2	4.3	9.5
Ultrasound	—	21.4	24.6	23.3
PET scanner	—	—	0.4	0.6
SPECT scanner	—	—	4.2	7.2
Transplant services	—	—	—	2.0
Kidney transplant	0.7	0.8	0.9	—
Other organ transplant	1.0	1.1	1.1	—
Tissue transplant	—	—	1.2	—
Bone marrow transplant	—	—	0.7	—
Lithotripter	—	0.2	1.4	3.1

Note: Data on ownership are from the American Hospital Association Annual Survey. The maximum number of units per million is 31.4 in 1980, 29.5 in 1985, 27.3 in 1990, and 24.5 in 1995.

catheterization, open-heart surgery, angioplasty, megavoltage radiation, stereotactic radiosurgery, CT scanners, MRIs, PET scanners, SPECT scanners, transplant services, and lithotripters. The other technologies (radioactive implants, therapeutic radioisotopes, X-ray therapy, and diagnostic radioisotopes) we classify as already diffused.

In addition to the distinction between diffusing and already-diffused technologies, we also have variation within the diffusing technologies in time of introduction. For example, angioplasty was about as diffused in 1990 as cardiac catheterization was in 1980; SPECT scanners in 1990 were about as diffused as CT scanners in 1980. Thus, we can look at how managed care has changed over time the diffusion of technologies in the same state of overall diffusion.

To examine the relation between managed-care enrollment and technology adoption in 1980, we estimate models similar to our previous analysis:

$$\left(\frac{Units}{Million}\right)_s = \beta_1 HMO\ Enrollment_s + X_s\ \beta + \varepsilon_s,\quad (3.3)$$

where s indexes states. As control variables (X), we include the logarithm of per capita income in the state, the percentage of the population living in urban areas, and the logarithm of state population.[17] As before, all regressions are weighted by state population.

The first column of table 3.11 shows estimates of equation (3.3). We report only the coefficient on the HMO enrollment variable. In general, the other variables are as we would expect: States with higher incomes have increased technology diffusion, and more-urban areas have less technology diffusion (reflecting shorter commuting times). As population increases, so does the number of units of technology per million.

The table's first row shows that for all of the technologies, HMO enrollment has a positive but statistically insignificant effect on technology diffusion. Each ten-percentage-point increase in HMO enrollment raises the ownership of the average technology by 0.2 units per million people. The next two rows show that this effect is very different for the diffusing technologies relative to those already diffused. Among the diffusing technologies, HMO enrollment is associated with more technology ownership. The coefficient is positive and statistically significant. Among already diffused technologies, in contrast, HMO

---

17. We experimented with other population characteristics but found they were not significantly related to technology ownership.

Table 3.11
Effect of managed care on technology adoption

Technology	1980 HMO enrollment	1990 HMO enrollment	1990 Technology leader	1995 HMO enrollment	1995 Technology leader
All	1.96 (1.67)	-3.93 (1.14)	1.03 (0.15)	-6.13 (1.53)	0.99 (0.23)
New technologies	6.19 (1.43)	-2.73 (0.91)	0.85 (0.12)	-5.40 (1.37)	0.89 (0.20)
Old technologies	-4.39 (3.42)	-7.28 (3.31)	1.54 (0.42)	-8.30 (4.17)	1.32 (0.62)
Cardiac					
Catheterization	6.31 (3.08)	-7.52 (3.18)	1.50 (0.41)	-6.75 (0.31)	1.06 (0.46)
Open-heart surgery	6.13 (3.34)	-2.21 (1.99)	1.47 (0.25)	-3.59 (1.97)	1.37 (0.29)
Angioplasty	—	-5.38 (2.72)	1.71 (0.35)	-4.32 (2.45)	1.24 (0.36)
Radiation therapy	—	—	—	-4.60 (2.58)	0.41 (0.38)
Megavoltage radiation	-1.30 (3.13)	-5.12 (2.61)	0.68 (0.33)	—	—
Radioactive implants	-0.37 (2.73)	-5.71 (2.70)	1.27 (0.34)	—	—
Therapeutic radioisotope	-8.14 (3.68)	-5.46 (2.93)	0.67 (0.37)	—	—
X-ray therapy	-4.26 (4.01)	-4.47 (2.67)	0.87 (0.34)	—	—
Stereotactic radiosurgery	—	-0.82 (1.13)	0.53 (0.14)	—	—

Technology	1980	1990		1995	
	HMO enrollment	HMO enrollment	Technology leader	HMO enrollment	Technology leader
Diagnostic radiology					
CT scanner	22.18 (5.67)	-12.90 (5.92)	2.20 (0.75)	-12.00 (5.25)	2.22 (0.78)
Diagnostic radioisotope	-4.78 (1.05)	-10.14 (5.77)	1.57 (0.74)	-9.78 (4.09)	0.29 (0.65)
MRI	—	-0.07 (2.68)	0.98 (0.34)	-9.15 (3.52)	1.78 (0.52)
Ultrasound	—	-10.64 (8.50)	3.34 (1.08)	-10.53 (7.58)	3.25 (1.13)
PET scanner	—	-0.66 (0.79)	0.16 (0.10)	-1.48 (0.61)	0.26 (0.09)
SPECT	—	-2.14 (3.49)	0.56 (0.45)	-7.18 (3.20)	-0.10 (0.47)
Transplant services	—	—	—	—	-0.15 (0.42)
Kidney transplant	0.63 (1.20)	-1.15 (0.97)	0.52 (0.12)	-1.65 (2.83)	—
Organ transplant	3.18 (1.93)	2.40 (2.82)	0.40 (0.36)	—	—
Tissue transplant	—	-2.65 (1.45)	0.64 (0.18)	—	—
Bone marrow transplant	—	0.11 (0.82)	0.17 (0.10)	—	—
Lithotripter	—	-0.08 (0.18)	0.32 (0.23)	-2.48 (2.46)	0.30 (0.37)

Note: The table shows regressions of technology ownership per million population on HMO enrollment in the state and, for 1990 and 1995, the state's technology leadership in 1980. Regressions also include controls for the logarithm of per capita income, the percentage of the state's population living in urban areas, and the logarithm of the state's population. Regressions are weighted by state population. The first three rows include dummy variables for the different technologies.

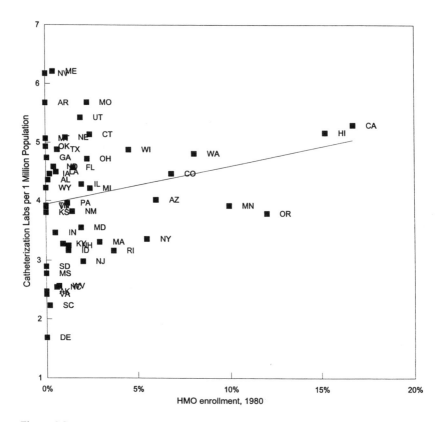

Figure 3.9
HMO enrollment and the diffusion of cardiac catheterization labs, 1980

enrollment has an insignificant negative effect on the ownership of technology.

The insignificant effect of HMOs on already-diffused technologies suggests that HMO enrollment is not associated with long-run differences in technology availability across states. This makes sense; technologies available for some time have spread more or less equally among all states. But states with high HMO enrollment in 1980 are technology leaders—new technologies are more common there than in other states.

Figure 3.9 shows this graphically by depicting the relation between HMO enrollment and cardiac catheterization units in 1980. States like California and Hawaii, leaders in managed-care enrollment, also have high numbers of catheterization units. HMO enrollment is positively correlated with catheterization labs.

We want to know how the HMO coefficient changes over time. If managed care is reducing the diffusion of new technologies, the HMO coefficient should fall in the later years of the sample. There is a problem, however, in simply estimating equation (3.3) for different years. Our results for 1980 suggest that some states are naturally technology leaders and others are technology "followers." If we want to look at managed care's effect on technology diffusion, we need to control for whether the state is a technology leader.[18] That is, we need to modify equation (3.3) to:

$$\left(\frac{Units}{Million}\right)_s = \beta_1 HMO\ Enrollment_s + \beta_2 Technology\ Leader_s + x_s\,\beta + \varepsilon_s\,. \quad (3.4)$$

Here, β_1 gives HMO enrollment's effect on technological availability, controlling for the fact that some states are naturally leaders and others are followers.

There is clearly no variable for technology leadership. But our data suggest a natural proxy: We take all of the diffusing technologies in 1980 and normalize the ownership variables so that they have a mean of zero and a standard deviation of one.[19] We then add the normalized ownership measures across the different technologies. The result is a measure of the state's propensity to own high-tech medical services in 1980, which we use as a proxy for technology leadership.

The second through fifth columns of table 3.11 show estimates of equation (3.4) in 1990 and 1995. We report only the coefficients on HMO enrollment and the technology leadership variable, although the logarithm of per capita income, the share of the state living in urban areas, and the logarithm of state population are also included in the regression.

Increased HMO enrollment is associated with less-rapid diffusion of new technologies in 1990 and 1995, and this effect is increasing over time. As the first row shows, states that were technology leaders in 1980 are more likely to adopt new technologies in the 1990s. The coefficient on the leadership variable is positive and statistically

---

18. In examining the managed care's impact on technology adoption, Chernew, Fendrick, and Hirth (1997) examined whether a new gallbladder surgery, laparoscopic cholecystectomy, diffused more slowly within HMOs. They found little difference between HMOs and the general population in the rate of growth in utilization. However, they were not able to control for this "leader effect," which might have led to their results.

19. That is, we form $z_s = (units/million_s - \mu)\,/\,\sigma$, where μ is the mean ownership across states and σ is the standard deviation.

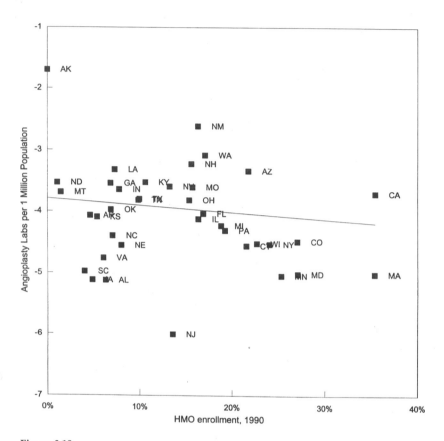

Figure 3.10
HMO enrollment and the diffusion of angioplasty labs, 1990

significant. Conditional on this effect, however, increased HMO enrollment significantly reduces the propensity of states to adopt new technologies. Further, the coefficient on HMO enrollment is more negative
in 1995 than in 1990, suggesting that HMO enrollment is increasingly
affecting the diffusion of new technologies over time. This finding is
not just a result of the fact that technologies are on average older in the
1990s than in 1980. Even for the new technologies of the late 1980s and
early 1990s, such as angioplasty, PET scanners, SPECT scanners, and
lithotripters, the coefficients on HMO enrollment are generally negative and often statistically significant.

Figure 3.10 shows one particular example graphically by depicting
the relation between HMO enrollment in 1990 and the number of
angioplasty units per million people. Angioplasty in 1990 is roughly

the technological equivalent to cardiac catheterization in 1980; both are procedures used in the treatment of severe coronary problems. Thus, the comparison between figures 3.9 and 3.10 implicitly reveals HMOs' effect on similar technologies over time. As figure 3.10 shows, there is essentially no relation between HMO enrollment and angioplasty units. Even though the high managed-care states in 1980 are generally the high managed-care states in 1990, those states are not the ones where technology is diffusing most rapidly. California, for example, is only average in angioplasty units, and Massachusetts, another high HMO state, is below average. When we control for the fact that these states were technology leaders in 1980, our regressions in table 3.11 indicate a negative and statistically significant effect of managed care on technology diffusion.

In principle, managed care might affect different types of technologies differently. Technologies that save money might be adopted more readily in heavy managed-care states, whereas technologies that add to costs should diffuse less rapidly. We find it difficult to analyze this in our data, however; a more systematic study of this issue would be needed to reach firm conclusions.

VI. Conclusion

The differences across states in the pervasiveness of managed care has allowed us to examine managed care's effects on health care systems—looking not only at the insurance premiums those in managed care pay or the reimbursement providers receive from managed-care companies but at managed care's total impact on health expenditures. The results are fairly encouraging.[20] The higher is HMO enrollment in a state, the lower is the growth of hospital spending. Over the entire 1980–93 period, an equal increase in physician and drug spending almost negated the reduction in hospital cost growth. However, in 1988–93, the increase in physician spending was much more muted, and managed care reduced the growth rate not only of hospital spending, but of spending overall.

Managed care's impact on physician spending was a surprise to us, and it warrants further investigation. Its impact on hospitals was more in line with anecdotal evidence—managed care reduced hospital costs

---

20. Of course, without a measure of health outcomes, it is impossible to determine whether managed care is worth its cost.

primarily by reducing the length of stay in the hospital, leading to fewer hospital employees per person as well as fewer hospital beds.

Perhaps more important than the finding that managed care reduces health spending overall is the preliminary evidence that managed care may also slow the rate of adoption of new technologies. States with high enrollment in HMOs used to be the first to adopt new technologies; now, they are only average. Because rapid adoption of new technology is believed to be one of the main factors behind the rise in health expenditures, the finding that HMOs can reduce technology adoption means that managed care may actually moderate the long-term growth of health expenditures. That is a subject well worth further investigation.

References

Aaron, Henry. 1991. *Serious and Unstable Condition: Financing America's Health Care.* Washington, DC: The Brookings Institution.

Baker, Lawrence C. 1997. "The Effect of HMOs on Fee-for-Service Health Care Expenditures: Evidence from Medicare." *Journal of Health Economics* 16(4):453–481.

Chernew, Michael, A. Mark Fendrick, and Richard A. Hirth. 1997. "Managed Care and Medical Technology: Implications for Cost Growth." *Health Affairs* 16(2) (March/April):196–206.

Cutler, David M., and Mark McClellan. 1996. "The Determinants of Technological Change in Heart Attack Treatments." NBER Working Paper No. 5751, September 1996.

Gabel, Jon. 1997. "Ten Ways HMOs Have Changed during the 1990s." *Health Affairs* 16(3) (May/June):134–45.

Gabel, Jon, Cindy Jajich-Toth, Gregory de Lissovoy, Thomas Rice, and Howard Cohen. 1988. "The Changing World of Group Health Insurance." *Health Affairs* 7(3) (summer):48–65.

Holahan, John, and David Liska. 1997. "The Slowdown in Medicaid Spending Growth: Will It Continue?" *Health Affairs* 16(2) (March/April):157–63.

Jensen, Gail A., et al., 1997. "The New Dominance of Managed Care Insurance: Trends in the 1990s." *Health Affairs* 16(1) (January/February):148–156.

Krueger, Alan B., and Helen Levy. 1997. "Accounting for the Slowdown in Employer Health Care Costs." "National Tax Association Proceedings," 61–75.

Levit, Katharine R., Helen C. Lazenby, Cathy A. Cowan, Darleen K. Won, Jean M. Stiller, Lekha Sivarajan, and Madie W. Stewart. 1995. "State Health Expenditure Accounts: Building Blocks for State Health Spending Analysis." *Health Care Financing Review* 17(1) (fall)201–54.

Melnick, Glenn, and Jack Zwanziger. 1995. "State Health Care Expenditures under Competition and Regulation, 1980 through 1991." *American Journal of Public Health* 85(10) (October):1391–6.

Newhouse, Joseph P. 1992. "Medical Care Costs: How Much Welfare Loss?" *Journal of Economic Perspectives,* 6(3) (Summer):3–21.

Newhouse, Joseph P., and the Insurance Experiment Group. 1993. *Free For All? Lessons from the Rand Health Insurance Experiment.* Cambridge, MA: Harvard University Press.

Reinhardt, Uwe. 1996. "Our Obsessive Quest to Gut the Hospital." *Health Affairs* 15(3) (summer):145–54.

Simon, Carol, and Patricia Born. 1996. "Physician Earnings in a Changing Managed Care Environment." *Health Affairs* 15(4) (fall):124–33.

Simon, Carol, and David W. Emmons. 1997. "Physician Earnings at Risk: An Examination of Capitated Contracts." *Health Affairs* 16(3) (May/June):134–45.

Wholey, Douglas, Roger Feldman, and Jon Christianson. 1995. "The Effect of Market Structure on HMO Premiums." *Journal of Health Economics* 14(1):81–105.

Wickizer, Thomas M., and Paul J. Feldstein, 1995. "The Impact of HMO Competition on Private Health Insurance, 1985–1992." *Inquiry* 32(3):241–252.

Zwanziger, Jack, and Glenn Melnick. 1996. "Can Managed Care Plans Control Health Care Costs?" *Health Affairs* 15(3) (summer):185–99.

4

Managed Care and Health Care Expenditures: Evidence from Medicare, 1990–1994

Laurence C. Baker, *Stanford University and NBER*
Sharmila Shankarkumar, *Stanford University*

Executive Summary

Increases in the activity of managed care organizations may have "spillover effects," influencing the entire health care delivery system's performance, so that care for both managed-care and non–managed-care patients is affected. Some proposals for Medicare reform have incorporated spillover effects as a way that increasing Medicare HMO enrollment could contribute to savings for Medicare.

This paper investigates the relationship between HMO market share and expenditures for the care of beneficiaries enrolled in traditional fee-for-service Medicare. We find that increases in systemwide HMO market share (which includes both Medicare and non-Medicare enrollment) are associated with declines in both Part A and Part B fee-for-service expenditures. The fact that managed care can influence expenditures for this population, which should be well insulated from the direct effects of managed care, suggests that managed-care activity can have broad effects on the entire health care market. Increases in Medicare HMO market share alone are associated with increases in Part A expenditures and with small decreases in Part B expenditures. This suggests that any spillovers directly associated with Medicare HMO enrollment are small.

For general health care policy discussions, these results suggest that assessment of new policies that would influence managed care should account not only for its effects on enrollees but also for its systemwide effects. For Medicare policy discussions, these findings imply that previous results that seemed to show large spillover effects associated with increases in Medicare HMO market share, but inadequately accounted for systemwide managed-care activity and relied on older data, overstated the magnitude of actual Medicare spillovers.

We thank David Cutler, Alan Garber, and Mark McClellan for helpful suggestions regarding this research. Address correspondence to Laurence Baker, Department of Health Research and Policy, HRP Redwood Building, Rm 253, Stanford University School of Medicine, Stanford, CA 94305-5405

I. Introduction

As managed care's influence grows, understanding its influence on the structure and functioning of the health care marketplace is increasingly important. During recent years, a number of studies have examined the hypothesis that managed-care activity may broadly affect the entire health care system through so-called spillover effects. These studies argue that managed-care organizations may, among other things, compete with non–managed-care providers or insurers, influence the systemwide availability of new technologies or other health care services, influence the structure of hospital markets, and contribute to the spread of conservative practice patterns among non–managed-care providers, all of which contribute to changes in provider behavior and health care costs throughout the health care system.

Whether managed care can have widespread effects on health care delivery and costs is important for assessing the effects of the health care system's ongoing transformation on health care costs and patient care and for evaluating policies that would encourage or discourage growth in managed care. In particular, most analyses of managed care have focused on patients enrolled in managed care plans, but the presence of spillover effects would imply the need to include consideration of non–managed-care enrollees as well.

This chapter investigates the relationship between systemwide managed care activity and expenditures for the care of patients covered by Medicare's traditional fee-for-service (FFS) plan. These patients should be well insulated from managed care's direct effects, so that studying their expenditures provides a strong test of managed care's ability to influence care for non–managed-care patients. FFS Medicare is a well-defined, stable insurance plan that does not subject patients to the limitations managed care plans typically impose. There is little or no central management of provider or patient utilization choices (i.e., utilization review). It imposes no strong financial incentives on providers to limit utilization. Physicians caring for Medicare FFS patients are paid on a fee-for-service basis, subject only to limitations on the fees for individual services embodied in the Medicare Fee Schedule. Hospitals are paid using diagnosis-related groups (DRGs). Although DRGs do impose some incentives for cost containment, they are among the weaker incentives used to influence hospitals in today's health care system and, in fact, some work has shown that DRGs do vary with treatment intensity, so that the incentive for hospitals to reduce intensity to contain costs is not complete (McClellan 1997). In addition, the

Medicare FFS program does not compete for patients, and the competitive forces that increasingly pervade the overall health care system therefore do not influence it. Overall, because FFS Medicare patients should be well outside the boundaries of managed care, any effect of managed care on their expenditures may be taken as clear evidence of managed care's power to transform the health care system fundamentally in ways that affect all patients.

Focusing on Medicare expenditures also allows us to investigate issues related to Medicare policy. Spillover effects that affect Medicare spending have attracted particular interest in Medicare reform discussions because policy changes that would increase HMO enrollment among Medicare beneficiaries could produce spillovers, reducing Medicare costs and contributing to the savings needed to restore balance in Medicare financing. The key question is whether changes in Medicare HMO activity can themselves bring about savings through spillover effects. Although most examinations of spillover effects focus on managed-care activity throughout the health care system, the existence of expenditure-reducing spillover effects induced by HMO activity outside of Medicare need not imply that changes in Medicare HMO activity also produce savings. Existing studies that look specifically at Medicare HMO market share have not fully answered this question, because they have not clearly identified the effects of Medicare HMO enrollment separately from systemwide HMO effects. This chapter studies Medicare HMO market share's effect on expenditures, controlling for changes in systemwide HMO activity.

A number of previous studies have examined spillover effects from various perspectives (e.g., Goldberg and Greenberg 1979; Frank and Welch 1985; Feldman et al. 1986; Luft et al. 1986; Dowd 1987; McLaughlin 1987, 1988; Noether 1988; Robinson 1991, 1996; Baker 1994; Chernew 1995; Baker and Corts 1996). Although these studies contribute to our understanding of spillover effects, data limitations have left them generally unable to draw clear, broad-based conclusions about systemwide managed-care activity's impact on non—managed-care patients. Some of these studies have been forced to rely on data about managed care from only a small number of markets. Many have also had to rely on expenditure data from single sectors of the health care market (e.g., only from hospitals), which makes generalization difficult, or have had to lump together spending by managed-care and non–managed-care patients, which makes it difficult to separate spillover effects from managed care organizations' effects on the care provided to enrollees. This chapter uses detailed nationwide data on

HMO market share along with ambulatory and hospital expenditures for a well-defined group of FFS patients to overcome these difficulties.

Four studies have examined Medicare data for evidence of spillovers. Baker (1997) examined data on Medicare HMO enrollment and FFS expenditures between 1986 and 1990, finding that increases in Medicare market share from 10 to 20% were associated with decreases of 4.5 and 4.1% in FFS expenditures for hospital and physician services, respectively. Welch (1994) found a negative relationship between Medicare risk HMO market share and aggregate (HMO and non-HMO) Medicare expenditures per beneficiary between 1984 and 1987. Clement, Gleason, and Brown (1992) used data from 1985–88 and estimated that increases of ten percentage points in Medicare risk HMO market share were associated with 5% decreases in Medicare FFS expenditures, although the results were sensitive to specification. Finally, Rodgers and Smith (1995) reported that increases in Medicare risk HMO market share were associated with decreases in FFS expenditures between 1988 and 1992. Although these studies offer insights into the existence of spillover effects in general, their main shortcoming is that they tend to focus only on Medicare HMO market share[1] and have been unable to clearly distinguish Medicare-specific spillovers from systemwide spillovers. Nonetheless, some have interpreted their results to imply that increases in Medicare HMO market share would lead to declines in Medicare FFS spending (e.g., Rodgers and Smith 1995; Hammonds 1997). In this chapter, we include both systemwide and Medicare-specific HMO market share to disentangle these two effects and evaluate this conclusion.

The remainder of this chapter proceeds as follows. The next section discusses how managed care may be expected to influence expenditures and the issues raised when examining managed-care spillovers in Medicare. Section III discusses estimation issues and presents results, and section IV concludes.

II. HMOs and Health Care Expenditures

Mechanisms

The term "managed care," in popular parlance, is often poorly defined and can refer to a wide variety of health care organizations. In this

---

1. Rodgers and Smith (1995) do include some data on systemwide HMO market share but are forced to rely on a limited sample of 89 metropolitan areas.

chapter, we use this term to refer conceptually to organizations that take an active role in limiting the providers their patients can use (e.g., through selective contracting), that use financial incentives designed to limit utilization (e.g., capitation), and/or that actively limit patient utilization through other means (e.g., utilization review). This is a purposefully broad set of criteria designed to capture the spirit of recent changes in the health care marketplace. Although this framework guides conceptual development, practical considerations constrain the empirical work described below to focus only on HMOs.

Managed care may influence FFS expenditures through a variety of mechanisms. First, increases in managed-care activity may change the health care delivery system's structure and capacity. For example, managed care may change the incentives associated with the purchase of high-cost medical technologies, affecting technology availability in markets (Baker and Wheeler 1997; Cutler and Sheiner 1997). Similar effects could result if managed care changes the structure of the hospital market, the size or behavior of individual hospitals (e.g., Chernew 1995), the number and type of health care providers (Baker and Brown 1997), or other market characteristics. By changing the environment in which medicine is practiced, managed care may influence the type and costs of care provided to all patients.

Managed care may also influence health care providers' behavior, independent of any effects it may have on the overall availability of services. For example, in markets with high levels of managed-care activity, all providers may be less likely to use procedures perceived to have high ratios of costs to benefits. This could occur through a variety of mechanisms. If, as some models of physician learning suggest (e.g., Phelps 1992), physicians tend to adopt the practice patterns of other physicians around them, increases in the number of managed-care physicians practicing in a given area may result in faster promulgation of conservative practice techniques. A related possibility is that physicians who see both managed care and FFS patients may adopt more conservative practice styles throughout their practices. Finally, increases in managed-care activity or other increases in the strength of managed-care organization vis-à-vis traditional providers and insurers may increase competitive pressure as non–managed-care providers and insurers compete with managed-care organizations for the business of employers and patients. Competition could force non–managed-care providers to change how they provide care or prompt insurers to expand utilization review and other oversight efforts, leading to changes in utilization. (It should be noted that competition could also be associated with increasing expenditures. For example, competition from managed-care plans may prompt FFS providers to compete on the basis of quality or technology. Or, if managed care pulls patients away from physicians, they may respond by inducing demand from or increasing charges to non–managed-care patients.[2])

A final mechanism by which managed-care activity could have spillover effects on FFS expenditures is price. If non–managed-care providers or insurers earn excess profits in the absence of managed care, increasing competition could enhance market discipline and lead to lower prices.

Observing Spillover Effects in Medicare Data

The Medicare program provides an excellent opportunity to observe many of the effects described above. In particular, changes in the health care system's structure and capacity and changes in utilization patterns should influence Medicare expenditures. Most health care providers and most hospitals care for both Medicare and non-Medicare patients. If, for example, managed-care activity reduces the number of MRI machines available in a market, then utilization of MRI for Medicare patients is likely to be influenced. Similarly, if providers adopt more conservative practice styles for their non-Medicare patients, Medicare FFS patients may also be treated more conservatively. Because Part B reimbursement is based on the number and type of procedures performed, Part B expenditures will vary with changes in utilization. Part A expenditures capture variation in the number of hospitalizations and some variation in in-hospital utilization, although the Prospective Payment System, which governs Part A payments, dampens the relationship between in-hospital utilization intensity and Part A expenditures.[3]

A word on the role of competition is important here. Although competition-driven changes in technology availability or utilization could easily influence the care Medicare beneficiaries receive, these

---

2. Physicians' willingness and ability to do this is a subject of debate. Some evidence (e.g., Mitchell, Wedig, and Cromwell 1989; Cromwell and Mitchell 1986) indicates that physicians can induce demand and may do so in response to reductions in demand or prices.
3. Note, however, that McClellan (1997) shows that substantial portions of the variance in hospital reimbursements under the prospective payment system can be explained by variation in procedure codes and outlier payments that reflect variation in utilization patterns, so that Part A expenditures reflect in-hospital intensity to at least some degree.

competitive effects are likely to arise from non-Medicare sectors of the health care market since competition for Medicare beneficiaries is unlikely to have a strong impact on behavior. Medicare does not compete for the business of the elderly and disabled and does not operate under the same incentives that face for-profit insurance companies and health care providers (Clement, Gleason, and Brown 1992). In addition, provider behavior with respect to pricing and utilization has only small effects on the prices that Medicare FFS beneficiaries pay for coverage and care.

Although utilization effects should show up in the Medicare data, the structure Medicare imposes on the payments made to physicians and hospitals severely limits the extent to which managed care–induced price changes can occur in Medicare. Since 1983, the Health Care Financing Administration (HCFA) has reimbursed hospitals using the Prospective Payment System, which significantly limits managed care–induced price variation in Part A expenditures. Similarly, in the early 1990s, HCFA began phasing in the Medicare Fee Schedule for reimbursement of physicians under Part B. This schedule limits managed care–induced variation in physician prices. Since the fee schedule was being phased in during the time period on which we focus, all data presented here are adjusted to reflect what payments would have been under the 1994 fee schedule, which further limits the effect that changes in prices over time could have on our data. However, it remains theoretically possible that price effects could appear in our data to the extent that managed care–induced changes in physician or hospital prices were incorporated into the Prospective Payment System or fee schedule payment rates, although we believe this effect is relatively weak.

Systemwide Spillovers versus Medicare-Specific Spillovers

For discussions of Medicare policy, it is important to distinguish between the effects of systemwide and Medicare-specific managed care activity. "Systemwide" managed-care activity includes changes in the size, market power, or other aspects of managed-care organizations' behavior throughout the health care system, possibly including the effects of increasing managed-care activity within Medicare. "Medicare-specific" managed-care activity captures changes in the enrollment in only the Medicare portion of managed-care organizations. Changes in expenditures induced by Medicare-specific managed-care activity occur because only Medicare managed-care activity changed, independent of any other changes in the managed-care market. Changes in systemwide managed care activity induce expenditure effects because the entire sector's influence has changed.

If spillovers occur because managed-care activity changes throughout the entire health care system, then changes in Medicare HMO enrollment that Medicare policy changes might bring about would produce spillover effects only to the extent that increases in Medicare HMO enrollment increase overall enrollment. Because Medicare enrollment is only a fraction of overall enrollment, this would limit the impact increases in Medicare enrollment could have through spillovers. On the other hand, if increases in Medicare HMO market share itself directly influences expenditures independent of systemwide changes in market share, savings obtained could be greater.

It is not clear that the effects of systemwide and Medicare-specific HMO market share should be the same. Systemwide changes in managed-care activity have broad latitude in how they influence expenditures. In fact, all of the spillover effect mechanisms identified above could plausibly begin with systemwide managed care changes. On the other hand, Medicare-specific spillovers have much more limited potential to have strong effects (Clement, Gleason, and Brown 1992; Baker 1997). There is little reason to believe that Medicare-specific activity would bring about large changes in the overall health care market's structure and capacity or have important competitive effects. Significant Medicare-specific effects could occur most plausibly through learning and related effects. For example, if providers who see elderly or disabled patients share information among themselves but not with other physicians more generally, then increases in Medicare managed-care activity could change the behavior of Medicare FFS providers independent of changes in the non-Medicare market.

Although understanding Medicare-specific spillover effects is crucial for Medicare policy, it is difficult to draw conclusions about the size of Medicare-specific spillover effects from previous work. Because systemwide and Medicare-specific spillovers need not be the same, inferences cannot reliably be drawn from studies of spillover effects outside of Medicare. Although some studies have examined the effects of Medicare HMO market share on expenditures (Baker 1997; Welch 1994; Clement, Gleason, and Brown 1992; Rodgers and Smith 1995), they have not typically included systemwide HMO activity. Since systemwide managed-care activity and Medicare HMO activity are correlated, the relationship between HMO market share and expenditures could capture the effects of both Medicare-specific and system-wide managed-care activity. One goal of this chapter is to apply new data to attempt to disentangle these effects.

III. Data

Medicare Expenditures

Data on Part A and Part B Medicare FFS expenditures and enrollment by county for all counties in the United States for 1990–94 were obtained from HCFA. The expenditure data include only expenditures made on behalf of FFS beneficiaries[4]—payments to HMOs and other providers for the care of HMO-enrolled beneficiaries are not included. The data also exclude expenditures Medicare does not cover, such as copayments, deductibles, payments made for services not covered by Medicare, and payments for services covered by Medigap insurance. To construct the county-level measures of spending, expenditures for each beneficiary are assigned to his or her county of residence, regardless of where the expenditures were incurred.

The Medicare Fee Schedule governing Medicare payments to physicians was phased in during the time period under study here. To ensure that this does not affect the findings, the HCFA Office of the Actuary has adjusted the data for each year to reflect what payments in each year would have been under the 1994 Medicare Fee Schedule. This adjustment virtually eliminates the (already small) possibility of observing managed care–induced changes in physician prices.

For our analyses, we aggregate the county-level data to produce measures of spending for Health Care Service Areas (HCSAs): groups of counties thought to approximate markets for health services (Makuc et al. 1991). There are 802 HCSAs in the United States, representing both urban and rural areas. We expect HCSAs to be superior to counties as a market definition, because many counties are too small to represent adequately markets for health care services.

Table 4.1 reports national average expenditures per beneficiary for 1990–94. In 1990, on average, Medicare spent $2,037 per beneficiary for

---

4. The sample includes expenditures for the elderly and disabled but excludes expenditures for patients with end-stage renal disease, who are also covered by Medicare but make up less than 1% of beneficiaries and tend to have distinct health needs.

Table 4.1
Mean nominal Medicare FFS expenditures per beneficiary, 1990–1994

Year	Part A	% change from previous year	Part B	% change from previous year
1990	$2,037 (574)	—	$1,233 (346)	—
1991	$2,152 (547)	5.6%	$1,273 (338)	3.2%
1992	$2,432 (557)	13.0%	$1,322 (324)	3.8%
1993	$2,616 (645)	7.6%	$1,397 (367)	5.7%
1994	$2,865 (701)	9.5%	$1,539 (361)	10.2%
% change 1990–94		40.6%		24.8%

Note: Standard errors in parentheses. Values shown are national averages.

Part A services and $1,233 per beneficiary for Part B services. By 1994, these amounts had risen to $2,865 and $1,539, increases of 40.6% and 24.8%, respectively.

Medicare HMO Market Shares

Although the arguments developed above apply to managed care broadly, we focus our analytical efforts on HMO market share. This follows previous work and is, in practice, the only variable for which we can obtain comparable data over time for relatively small geographic areas. County-level data on the number of Medicare Part A beneficiaries enrolled in HMOs for 1989–94 (including risk, cost, and HCPPs) were obtained from HCFA.[5] County-level HMO market shares are simply the ratio of the number of HMO enrollees to the number of beneficiaries in each county.

As above, we aggregate the county-level data to form measures of Medicare HMO market share for market areas. The top panel of table 4.2 presents summary statistics for area Medicare HMO market shares

5. Although some previous analyses have used only risk HMO enrollment, this does not capture HMO activity as broadly or accurately as HMO market share from all contract types. Moreover, focusing only on risk enrollment may induce bias because Medicare HMOs can choose annually whether to operate as risk or cost plans, and FFS expenditure levels are likely to influence this choice.

Table 4.2
Summary statistics for HMO market share measures

Year	Weighted mean	Unweighted					
		Mean	Standard deviation	25th percentile	Median	75th percentile	90th percentile
Medicare HMO market share							
1990	6.4	2.3	5.4	0.1	0.3	1.5	6.8
1991	5.7	2.1	4.8	0.1	0.3	1.4	5.6
1992	6.0	2.2	5.0	0.2	0.3	1.5	5.9
1993	6.8	2.4	5.6	0.2	0.4	1.5	6.6
1994	7.8	2.8	6.2	0.2	0.4	2.0	7.7
Systemwide HMO market share							
1990	15.1	5.9	8.1	0	2.5	8.8	16.2
1991	15.7	6.1	8.3	0	2.6	9.5	16.2
1992	16.7	6.7	8.8	0.2	3.2	10.3	17.4
1993	18.2	7.5	9.3	0.5	4.1	11.2	18.9
1994	20.5	9.0	9.9	1.4	5.7	13.4	22.5

Note: Sample size is 802 Health Care Services Areas per year. Weighted means reflect nationwide population averages—weighted Medicare market share measures are weighted by Medicare enrollment, and weighted systemwide market shares are weighted by county population.

by year. The first column presents means weighted by the number of Medicare beneficiaries in each market area to produce national averages. Between 1990 and 1994, mean Medicare HMO market share grew from 6.4% to 7.8%. Since 1994, Medicare HMO market share has continued to grow, reaching approximately 10% in 1996.

Figure 4.1 graphs the distribution of 1994 levels and 1990–94 changes in Medicare market shares. 1994 market shares in the sample range from 0 to 47%. Medicare market shares have a highly skewed distribution, as evidenced by the fact that the median market shares are all well below the means. Between 1990 and 1994, Medicare HMO market share changed little in most areas. Among market areas in the sample, 1990–94 changes ranged from --9% to +27%. There was some upward movement in HMO market share in some areas, but most experienced only very small changes in market share. In this sample 1.0 percent (N=8) had decreased of more than 5%, 4.2% (N=34) had increases of more than 5%, and 81% (N=650) had changes that fell between −1% and +1%.

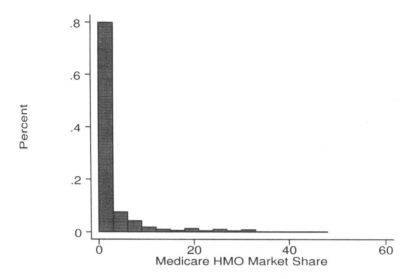

Figure 4.1a
Distribution of 1994 levels of Medicare HMO market share

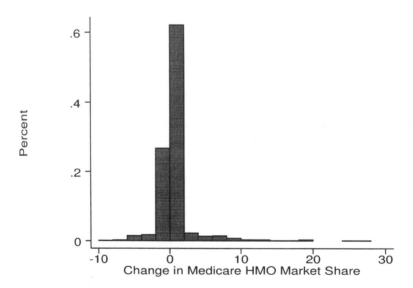

Figure 4.1b
1990–1994 changes in Medicare HMO market share
Note: Figures are based on 802 HCSAs each. Market areas are defined as HCSAs.

Systemwide HMO Market Shares

In addition to Medicare HMO market shares, we also incorporate estimates of systemwide (Medicare and non-Medicare) HMO market share. These estimates were constructed for previous studies using data from the Group Health Association of America (now called the American Association of Health Plans). Conceptually, construction took place in three steps. First, the total enrollment and service area, specified by county, of each HMO in the United States were obtained from annual surveys conducted by the GHAA that asked all known HMOs in the country about their total enrollment, county service area, and headquarters location. The results of the survey were published in the annual *National Directory of HMOs.*[6]

Next, the enrollment of each HMO was distributed among the counties in its service area. Initially, enrollment was simply distributed proportionally to county population. In addition, because HMO enrollment may be concentrated near HMO headquarters or because HMOs may locate their headquarters in areas where their enrollment is concentrated, estimates that incorporate both county population and distance from HMO headquarters were constructed. Estimates produced by the two methods have a correlation of approximately 0.97. Estimates that incorporate both population and distance were used in this study.

Finally, once enrollments had been distributed over service areas, the total number of enrollees in each county was computed by summing over the set of HMOs serving that county. Using the set of county enrollment estimates, market share estimates were computed as the proportion of the population enrolled in HMOs.

Since the county service areas on which the series are based are quite accurate, it is likely that the series themselves are also quite accurate. Nonetheless, use of any allocation mechanism that produces enrollment estimates will almost certainly lead to measurement error in some cases. Aggregating market shares to the HCSA level should

6. In general, compliance with the survey is quite good. In all five of the years taken together, fewer than ten HMOs (of a total of about 550 per year) failed to indicate their enrollment. Where data was missing, data from subsequent *Directories* was used. Most HMOs also indicated their service area. In 1990, 459 of 567 HMOs clearly indicated the counties that they served. Response rates improved over time, and by 1994, 566 of 572 HMOs reported their service area clearly. In cases where market area data was not available from the survey, market areas were determined by reference to subsequent *Directories* and/or telephone contact.

dampen the effects of any misestimation of market shares that may have occurred at the county level. Although geographically detailed independent data on HMO market share for the whole country for these years are not available, the estimates were compared to estimates for selected sets of metropolitan statistical areas from the GHAA for 1991 (Bergsten and Palsbo 1993) and from Interstudy for 1994 (Interstudy 1994). The estimates performed relatively well in these comparisons. In a few cases, the estimates were found to be at odds with the Interstudy estimates, and where the geographic allocation algorithm appeared to produce erroneous results, we adjusted the estimates to conform to the Interstudy estimates.

On average, systemwide HMO market shares rose from 15 to 21% between 1990 and 1994 (bottom panel of table 4.2). Within any given year, observed systemwide market shares were fairly widely distributed. For example, in 1994, observed market shares ranged from 0 to 54%. Figure 4.2(a) illustrates the distribution of systemwide HMO market shares across market areas in 1994. Between 1990 and 1994, systemwide HMO market shares rose in most areas. Figure 4.2(b) graphs the distribution of changes in systemwide market share for areas. Systemwide HMO market share changes in the sample range for 1990–94 from –14% to +22%. HMO market share declined in relatively few areas. About 1.0% ($N=8$) of the sample had declines of more than 5%. On the other hand, 27% ($N=219$) had increases of more than 5%.

An issue that becomes important as we attempt to disentangle the effects of systemwide and Medicare-specific HMO market share on Medicare expenditures is the extent to which the two measures are correlated. In cross sections for individual years, correlations between the market area estimates range from 0.52 to 0.54. The correlation between the 1990–94 changes in Medicare and systemwide market share is 0.25.

IV. Estimation

Background and Strategy

Our interest is in estimating the parameters of a function that relates FFS Medicare expenditures in a market to HMO market share in that market. Specifically,

$$E_i = f(S_i, M_i, X_i),$$
(4.1)

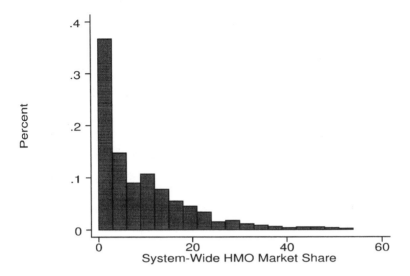

Figure 4.2a
Distribution of 1994 levels of systemwide HMO market share

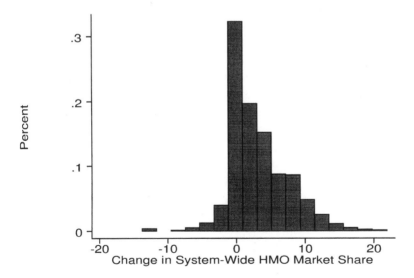

Figure 4.2b
1990–1994 changes in systemwide HMO market share

Note: Figures are based on 802 HCSAs each. Market areas are defined as HCSAs.

where E denotes Medicare FFS expenditures, M denotes Medicare-specific HMO activity, S denotes systemwide HMO activity, and X denotes other determinants of Medicare expenditures.

Several issues must be resolved to satisfactorily estimate equation (4.1). First, unobservable variables may be correlated with both market share and expenditures. For example, preferences of patients and providers for conservative care might increase HMO market share and decrease expenditures. Unobserved components of the population's health status may also influence both market share and expenditures. Although we control in the analyses for a number of potential confounding factors that we have been able to identify, we may not have identified all confounders. We attempt to solve this problem by including fixed effects in our models for areas and years. If the unobserved factors are constant within areas over time or are constant within years across areas, inclusion of the fixed effects removes any resulting bias from our estimates. In effect, this approach identifies the effects of HMO market share using changes within areas over time rather than variation in HMO activity across areas within individual years.

Second, HMO market share and expenditures may be simultaneously determined. Forward-looking HMOs may consider both current and expected future expenditures when deciding whether to enter or expand operations in a market. HMOs that can effectively reduce costs or utilization may be most successful in markets where FFS expenditures are high. Previous studies (e.g., Porell and Wallack 1990; Welch 1984; Goldberg and Greenberg 1981) have concluded that overall HMO market share is positively related to health care costs and utilization. Within the context of Medicare, the fact that payments to risk HMOs are dependent on FFS spending levels could also generate simultaneity bias. Areas with high FFS expenditures also have high risk HMO reimbursement rates, which may attract HMOs serving Medicare beneficiaries. If increases in FFS expenditures cause increases in HMO market share, then estimates of HMOs' effect on expenditures that do not account for simultaneity understate any expenditure-reducing effect HMOs may have.

We expect that the use of fixed effects in our analyses alleviates the difficulties associated with simultaneity to a large degree. Relying on changes over time to identify the effect of HMOs removes the bias induced by high expenditure levels causing high HMO market share levels. However, some bias could remain if expected future changes in expenditures prompt changes in market share. Previous work suggests that the conclusions drawn from fixed-effects models are broadly consistent with results from cross-sectional models that rely on instrumental variables to remove more fully simultaneity and omitted variables bias (Baker 1997). Further, given that previous work suggests that increases in expenditures should be associated with increases in HMO market share, any expenditure-reducing effects of HMO market share identified below can be interpreted as conservative to the extent that some simultaneity bias persists. Finally, any simultaneity bias induced through the Medicare risk HMO payment mechanism will influence only our estimates of the effects of Medicare-specific HMO enrollment; controlling for Medicare HMO market share should leave estimates of the effects of systemwide HMO activity unaffected by this source of bias.

Finally, the possibility of biased selection is an issue for estimation. Many studies have found that HMOs and other managed-care organizations receive a favorable selection of beneficiaries (see, among others, Hellinger 1987, 1995; Hill and Brown 1990). Given this evidence, selection bias is expected to associate increases in Medicare HMO market share with increases in FFS expenditures, because moving healthy beneficiaries into Medicare HMOs leaves the Medicare FFS population progressively sicker and therefore more expensive. Geographically detailed data on the characteristics of Medicare FFS and HMO beneficiaries are not available, so we are unable to control directly for the effects of biased selection. However, all of the relevant selection activity should occur with respect to Medicare HMOs, meaning that the Medicare HMO market share variables capture selection bias. Thus, controlling for Medicare HMO market share will leave our estimates of the effects of systemwide HMO market share unaffected by selection, but our estimates of the relationship between Medicare HMO market share and expenditures reflect selection bias as well as any spillover effects.

Results

We begin by estimating fixed-effects regression models of the form

$$\log(E_{i,t}) = \beta_0 + \beta_1 S_{i,t} + \beta_2 S^2_{i,t} + \beta_3 M_{i,t} + \beta_4 M_{i,t}{}^2 + \beta_5 \mathbf{X}_{i,t} \\ + \beta_6 A_i + \beta_7 Y_t + \varepsilon_{i,t},$$

(4.2)

where $\log(E)$ represents the natural logarithm of FFS expenditures per beneficiary, M represents Medicare HMO market share, S represents systemwide HMO market share, **X** is a vector of covariates expected to influence expenditures, A is a set of area-specific intercepts, and Y is a set of year-specific intercepts. The errors, $\varepsilon_{i,t}$, are assumed to be independently and identically distributed normal random variables. Subscript i denotes area i and subscript t denotes year t.

We estimate these models using current market share data. Most previous studies have used lagged data because HMO activity may have an effect on FFS expenditures only after a period of time. But because systemwide HMO market share estimates are available only for 1990–94, using current market share allows us to maximize the number of years in our sample. The year-to-year correlation in HMO market share is quite high, and estimation using lagged market shares and dropping 1990 data from the analysis does not significantly affect the estimates.

To capture changes in HMO market share's effect on expenditures as the level of HMO activity varies, equation (4.2) is quadratic in HMO market share. Previous work has explored various nonlinear functional forms and suggests that a quadratic specification adequately captures the relevant variation. We estimate equation (4.2) using our market area data, excluding the market area that contains Delta, Gunnison, Montrose, Hinsdale, Ouray, and San Miguel counties in Colorado, which experienced an implausibly high drop in systemwide HMO market share between 1990 and 1994, as well as Alaska and Hawaii. The final models use 801 observations per year ($N=4,005$).

We estimate separate models for Part A and Part B expenditures because differences in the content and reimbursement of ambulatory and hospital care may cause the effect of HMOs to vary. To correct for possible heteroskedasticity arising from variation in enrollments across markets and to maintain consistency with previous work, weighted least-squares regression was used, with Medicare Part A enrollment as the weight.

The control variables include per capita income; the proportions of the population aged 65–74, 75–84, and 85 and over; and the proportions of the over-65 population that are female, black, and "other race" (i.e., nonwhite and nonblack). To control for broad characteristics of the health care system that may influence expenditures, we include the number of physicians per 1,000 population and the number of hospital beds per 1,000 population. All these variables were obtained from the Census Bureau or from the Area Resource File, a dataset from the U.S. government Bureau of Health Professions that compiles health care data from a variety of sources including the AMA, the AHA, and the Census Bureau. The inclusion of area- and year-specific intercepts captures the effects of additional area- and year-specific unobserved or omitted variables.

Table 4.3 shows estimation results. Columns 1 and 4 present coefficients from the main specification. Note that the coefficients have been scaled to represent the effect of a ten-percentage-point change in market share (e.g., moving from 10% to 20% market share). To assess the statistical significance of the estimated relationships, F tests of the hypotheses that the linear and quadratic market share terms are jointly equal to zero were conducted separately for systemwide and Medicare market share. In all cases, the results were highly statistically significant.

For most practical purposes, we are concerned with the magnitude of the change in expenditures that would accompany a given change in market share. We estimate the percentage change in expenditures that would be associated with some representative changes in systemwide and Medicare HMO market share using the regression results. Specifically, the ratio of expenditures at system-wide market share $S2$ to expenditures at system-wide market share $S1$ can be estimated using:

$$E_{S2}/E_{S1} = \exp(\hat{\text{log}}E_{S2} - \hat{\text{log}}E_{S1})$$
$$= \exp(\hat{\beta}_1(S_2 - S_1) + \hat{\beta}_2(S_2^2 - S_1^2)). \tag{4.3}$$

where $\hat{\text{log}}E_{S1}$ and $\hat{\text{log}}E_{S2}$ are the predicted values of log (E) at systemwide market shares $S1$ and $S2$, respectively.[7] The quantity $(E_{S2}/E_{S1} - 1)$ can then be interpreted as the approximate percentage change in expenditures that would be associated with a move from market share $S1$ to $S2$. A similar equation can be used for Medicare market share changes, substituting the appropriate estimates from equation (4.2). The top panel of table 4.4 shows the estimated percentage changes in expenditures associated with moving systemwide HMO market share from 10 to 20, 20 to 30, and 30 to 40%. Estimates of the effect of moving HMO market share higher than 40 percent are not computed because there are relatively few sample points in that range.

Increases in systemwide HMO activity are associated with decreases in Part A expenditures. In the main specification (column 1), increases

---

7. Technically, this formula assumes that expenditures are log-normally distributed. Our analyses suggest that the Medicare data do approximately follow this distribution.

Table 4.3
Fixed-effects regression results using both systemwide and Medicare HMO market share, 1990–1994

Variables	Part A			Part B		
	All HCSAs (1)	HCSAs with greater than 1% market share (2)	MSA level (3)	All HCSAs (4)	HCSAs with greater than 1% market share (5)	MSA level (6)
Systemwide HMO market share /10	−0.012 (0.008)	−0.019 (0.010)	−0.022 (0.012)	−0.018 (0.005)	−0.016 (0.007)	−0.014 (0.008)
(Systemwide HMO market share /10)^2	−0.003 (0.001)	−0.001 (0.002)	−0.001 (0.002)	0.0003 (0.0010)	0.0002 (0.0012)	0.001 (0.001)
Medicare HMO market share /10	0.106 (0.012)	0.106 (0.014)	0.099 (0.017)	0.006 (0.008)	0.004 (0.009)	0.013 (0.012)
(Medicare HMO market share /10)^2	−0.004 (0.002)	−0.004 (0.003)	−0.006 (0.003)	−0.004 (0.002)	−0.004 (0.002)	−0.006 (0.002)
N	4005	2610	1610	4005	2610	1610
R^2	0.964	0.965	0.965	0.982	0.983	0.980
$F[df]$ (systemwide market share)	15.162 [2,3187]	11.077 [2,2071]	7.047 [2,1271]	15.808 [2,3187]	8.604 [2,2071]	2.555 [2,1271]
$P(F)$	0.000	0.000	0.001	0.000	0.000	0.078
$F[df]$ (Medicare market share)	92.751 [2,3187]	69.331 [2,2071]	39.473 [2,1271]	7.312 [2,3187]	5.741 2,2071]	5.860 [2,1271]
$P(F)$	0.000	0.000	0.000	0.001	0.003	0.003

Note: Standard errors are in parentheses. The dependent variable is the natural logarithm of expenditures per beneficiary. Regressions also contain controls for area population demographics, health system characteristics, year dummies, and an intercept. The F statistics shown test the hypotheses that the coefficients on the linear and quadratic market share terms are jointly zero. Regressions are weighted by Medicare enrollment.

Table 4.4
Percentage changes in Medicare FFS expenditures associated with selected representative changes in systemwide and Medicare HMO market share

Variables	Part A			Part B		
	All HCSAs (1)	HCSAs with greater than 1% market share (2)	MSA level (3)	All HCSAs (4)	HCSAs with greater than 1% market share (5)	MSA level (6)
Systemwide market share						
Moving from 10 to 20%	-1.9	-2.3	-2.3	-1.7	-1.5	-1.2
Moving from 20 to 30%	-2.5	-2.5	-2.4	-1.7	-1.5	-1.0
Moving from 30 to 40%	-3.0	-2.7	-2.5	-1.6	-1.4	-0.8
Medicare market share (independent)						
Moving from 10 to 20%	+9.4	+9.3	+8.2	-0.7	-0.8	-0.4
Moving from 20 to 30%	+8.5	+8.5	+7.1	-1.5	-1.6	-1.5
Moving from 30 to 40%	+7.7	+7.7	+6.0	-2.4	-2.4	-2.7
Medicare market share (total)						
Moving from 10 to 20%	+9.2	+9.1	+8.0	-0.9	-1.0	-0.6
Moving from 20 to 30%	+8.4	+8.3	+6.9	-1.7	-1.8	-1.7
Moving from 30 to 40%	+7.5	+7.5	+5.7	-2.6	-2.6	-2.8

Note: Values are based on regression coefficients shown in table 4.3.

in systemwide HMO market share from 10 to 20% are associated with 1.9% reductions in expenditures. Evaluated at the 1994 mean expenditure per beneficiary ($2,865), this corresponds to a decrease of $54.44. As HMO market share increases, an increase has a larger effect on expenditures. For example, increases in systemwide HMO market share from 20 to 30% are associated with 2.5% reductions in expenditures ($71.63 evaluated at the mean).

Increases in systemwide HMO market share are also associated with decreases in Part B expenditures (column 4). Increases in systemwide market share from 10 to 20% are associated with 1.7% decreases in expenditures. At mean 1994 expenditure levels ($1,539), this would correspond to a decrease of $26.16. Increases in HMO market share have weaker effects as HMO market share rises, but only to a limited degree. Increases in systemwide HMO market share from 20 to 30 or from 30 to 40% are associated with decreases of 1.7 and 1.6% percent, respectively, in Part B expenditures.

These findings are consistent with the hypothesis that systemwide HMO activity can influence the health care system in ways that affect expenditures for all patients. The evidence presented here is stronger than that found in previous studies because we have accounted for selection bias by including Medicare HMO market share as a control variable and for unobserved heterogeneity across markets by including market fixed effects.

Interpreting the results in tables 4.3 and 4.4 for Medicare-specific market share is less straightforward because the systemwide HMO market share variables include Medicare HMO market share along with non-Medicare HMO market share. To investigate the effect of a change in Medicare HMO market share independent of any effects of systemwide market share, we could use the regression coefficients β_3 and β_4 directly. But to assess fully the effects of a change in Medicare HMO market share, we must account for the effects of Medicare market share alone (through β_3 and β_4) as well as the effects of Medicare market share that occur through systemwide market share (captured in β_1 and β_2). Appendix A presents the equations necessary to do this. Table 4.4 summarizes the implied changes in expenditures associated with representative changes in market share using just the Medicare market share coefficients (the "independent" effect) and the implied changes in expenditures when both Medicare and systemwide effects are included (the "total" effect).

Increases in market share are associated with relatively large increases in Part A expenditures—independently, increases in Medicare HMO market share from 10 to 20% are associated with 9.4% increases in expenditures. Increases in market share are independently associated with decreases in Part B expenditures for market shares above about 7%. Increases in market share from 10 to 20% are associated with decreases of 0.7%. In both cases, the total effects are quite similar.

Drawing conclusions about the existence and magnitude of Medicare-specific spillover effects from these results is complicated by the fact that the coefficients capture the effects of biased selection and simultaneity, which are expected to associate increases in HMO market share with increases in expenditures, along with any expenditure-reducing spillovers. Thus, the results for Part A suggest that any spillover effects associated with Medicare HMO market share are much smaller than the effects of selection bias and simultaneity. For Part B, the results imply that there may be spillover effects large enough to offset the effects of selection bias and simultaneity.

To examine the robustness of the results, two alternate specifications of the basic equation were estimated. First, because many areas had very low Medicare HMO market shares, equation (4.2) was reestimated using only data from 522 HCSA market areas in which market share exceeded 1% in all years examined (columns 2 and 5 of tables 4.3 and 4.4). Second, equation (4.2) was reestimated using data at the metropolitan statistical area (MSA) level. MSAs are an alternative to HCSAs as a market definition and have been used by other authors, although they do not permit the inclusion of nonmetropolitan areas (columns 3 and 6 of tables 4.3 and 4.4). In both cases, the results are consistent with those reported above.

In addition to the models shown in tables 4.3 and 4.4, we tested several other specifications to examine the robustness of the results reported. We estimated equation (4.2) using unweighted least-squares regression, using lagged rather than current HMO market shares and dropping 1990, and excluding the number of short-term acute care hospital beds per 1,000 population and the number of physicians per 1,000 population in the area, because HMO market share may influence these variables, which could cause us to understate HMO activity's true effect. In all cases, the results were similar to the results initially obtained.

Comparison to Earlier Work

Four previous studies have examined the relationship between Medicare HMO market share and Medicare FFS expenditures. Table 4.5 summarizes the percentage changes in Medicare FFS expenditures estimated in these studies to accompany ten-percentage-point increases in Medicare market share. For Part A, previous studies suggested that expenditure decreases of 1.3 to 6.6% would accompany such increases, with most estimates toward the higher end of that range. For Part B, estimates ranged from 1.4 to 12.1% decreases. The results we present suggest that increases in Medicare HMO market share are associated with *increases* in Part A spending. The estimated declines in Part B spending that we report are generally much smaller than those reported in previous work.

Previous results and the results presented here could differ because our data is newer or because the model specified here differs from specifications in earlier studies (e.g., because we include both system-wide and Medicare market share). To present some information about

Table 4.5
Main estimates from previous studies of the percentage reductions in Medicare FFS spending accompanying ten-percentage-point increases in Medicare HMO market share

Study	Years examined	Part A expenditures	Part B expenditures	All expenditures
		Effect of a ten-percentage-point increase in Medicare HMO market share on		
Baker 1997	1986–90	−4.5, −6.6[a]	−4.1, −5.6[a]	—
Rodgers and Smith 1995	1988–92	−4.8[b]	−12.1[b]	−7.9[b]
Welch 1994	1986–87	−1.3[c]	−1.4[c]	−1.2[c]
Clement, Gleason, and Brown 1992	1985–88	−6[d]	−4[d]	−5[d]

[a]Baker (1997) estimated a nonlinear specification. Results shown here are for moves from 10 to 20 and from 20 to 30% market share, respectively.
[b]These figures are taken from the "Net HMO penetration rate effect" row in table 7 of the study.
[c]These are Welch's short-run estimates. He argues that the long-run effects of a change in market share may be much larger. Only the estimate for Part B expenditures is statistically significant at the $p=0.05$ level. (The estimate for all expenditures is significant at the $p=0.10$ level.)
[d]These are the main results, as transmitted in the project's final report. Other specifications presented in the paper produce a range of similar results.

these two alternatives, we have estimated two additional models. First, we replicated the specification used above eliminating the systemwide HMO market share variables. Columns 1 and 3 of table 4.6 show these results. Here, the implied increases in Part A expenditures are somewhat smaller than those observed with systemwide HMO market share included (cf. table 4.4). For Part B expenditures, the results suggest larger declines in expenditures. Together these results suggest that when systemwide HMO market share is omitted from the specification, the Medicare HMO market share variables capture some of its expenditure-reducing effect and may overstate the size of associated cost decreases or understate the size of associated cost increases.

Table 4.6
Fixed-effects regression results from models with only Medicare HMO market share, 1990–1994

Variables	Part A		Part B	
	Replicate table 4.3 (1)	Replicate Baker 1997 (2)	Replicate table 4.3 (3)	Replicate Baker 1997 (4)
Regression coefficients				
Medicare HMO market share /10	0.096 (0.012)	0.064 (0.008)	−0.0002 (0.0080)	−0.037 (0.005)
(Medicare HMO market share /10)^2	−0.004 (0.002)	−0.003 (0.002)	−0.004 (0.002)	−0.001 (0.001)
N	4005	15370	4005	15370
R^2	0.964	0.952	0.982	0.976
$F[df]$ (market share)	79.84 [2, 3189]	78.99 [2, 12283]	12.22 [2, 3189]	101.63 [2, 12283]
$P(F)$	0.000	0.000	0.000	0.000
Implied percentage changes in expenditures from representative changes in HMO market share				
Moving from 10 to 20%	+8.3	+5.4	−1.2	−3.8
Moving from 20 to 30%	+7.4	+4.8	−2.0	−4.0
Moving from 30 to 40%	+6.6	+4.1	−2.9	−4.1

Note: Standard errors are in parentheses. The dependent variable is the natural logarithm of expenditures per beneficiary. Columns 1 and 3 replicate the specification used in table 4.3, except that systemwide HMO market share is excluded. Columns 2 and 4 replicate the specification used in Baker 1997. In columns 2 and 4, Medicare HMO market share is lagged one year. Regressions also contain controls for area population demographics, year dummies, and an intercept. Regressions in columns 1 and 3 also include physicians and hospital beds per capita. The F statistics shown test the hypotheses that the coefficients on the linear and quadratic market share terms are jointly zero. Regressions are weighted by Medicare enrollment.

To investigate the effect of using newer data, we have also replicated the specification used in Baker 1997, which included only Medicare HMO market share and was originally run using data from 1986–90, using our data from 1990–94. This specification is similar to that used above but differs in three ways: The models are estimated at the county, rather than the HCSA, level;[8] lagged HMO market share is used instead of current; and the variables measuring the number of physicians and hospital beds per capita are not included. Columns 2 and 4 of table 4.6 present results. Here, increases in Medicare market share from 10 to 20% are associated with 5.4% increases in Part A expenditures. Results using data from 1986–90 showed that Part A expenditures fell by 4.5% for the same increase in market share. Comparing these results suggests that the relationship between HMO market share and expenditures may have changed over time and that the differences between the findings reported above and those in previous studies may stem both from changes in the specifications and changes over time. For Part B expenditures, 1990–94 data imply that increases in HMO market share from 10 to 20% are associated with declines of 3.8% percent, whereas 1986–90 data implied that increases in market share from 10 to 20% were associated with 4.0% decreases. These results suggest that, for Part B, the differences between the findings here and the earlier findings are more closely related to changes in the specification and the inclusion of systemwide market share than to changes over time.

An Alternate Specification

The models described above rely on changes in HMO market share and expenditures over time to identify the effects of HMO market share. Although this approach has powerful statistical properties, allows us to incorporate five years of data, and is consistent with previous studies, it does not incorporate the baseline levels of expenditures and HMO market share. Thus, it does not permit us to investigate the possibility that initial levels of HMO activity may influence the subsequent growth rate of expenditures. If areas with initially high levels of HMO market shares had slower expenditure growth, for

---

8. We exclude from the analyses counties with fewer than 50 beneficiaries in any of the years. The final sample included 3,074 counties per year ($N=15{,}370$).

example, fixed-effects models that essentially difference out the baseline market share levels would not capture this effect. Of particular concern is the possibility that initial levels of HMO market share may also be associated with the subsequent growth rate of HMO market share.[9] If initial HMO market share is associated with both expenditure growth and HMO market share growth, then fixed-effects models may lead to inaccurate estimates of the effects of changes in HMO activity.

To account for both initial levels of HMO activity and changes over time, we estimate first-differenced models of the form

$$\log(E_{i,94}) - \log(E_{i,90}) = \beta_0 + \beta_1 S_{i,90} + \beta_2 (S_{i,94} - S_{i,90}) + \beta_3 M_{i,90}$$
$$+ \beta_4 (M_{i,94} - M_{i,90}) + \beta_5 Q1_{i,90} + \beta_6 Q4_{i,90} \qquad (4.4)$$
$$+ \beta_7 X_{i,90} + \beta_8 (X_{i,94} - X_{i,90}) + \eta_i .$$

That is, this specification models the difference in log expenditures between 1990 and 1994, which is approximately equal to the percentage change in expenditures over that time, as a function of the initial levels of HMO market share and the 1990–94 changes in market share. We include in X the same set of covariates as above to control for population and health system characteristics, and we add the percentage of the population in each market that lives in an urban area to capture urban-rural differences.

Equation (4.4) is estimated using the market area (HCSA) data. As above, we exclude Alaska, Hawaii, and the Colorado HCSA that appears to have inaccurate systemwide HMO market share data. We do not include quadratic terms in the market shares, because this makes the equation unwieldy and does not add substantially to the conclusions. We weight the regressions using the 1990 Medicare HMO enrollment in each market area.

A potential difficulty with estimating equation (4.4) is that in areas with particularly high or low expenditures in a given year, expenditures may regress to the mean over time. For example, if an area has high expenditures in one year because of particularly bad health outcomes in its population, it is likely to have lower health expenditures in subsequent years because the health outcomes the area population experiences are likely to fall more near the mean.[10] If managed-care

---

9. The observed (weighted) correlation between the 1990 systemwide market share and the 1990–94 change is 0.23; for Medicare market share, the correlation is 0.41.

10. The observed (weighted) correlations between the log of mean 1990 expenditures and the 1990–94 changes in log expenditures are –0.36 for Part A and –0.64 for Part B.

organizations disproportionately locate in high-expenditure areas, then the resulting association between HMO market share and subsequent regression to the mean in expenditures could produce biased estimates of HMO's effects. The variables $Q1$ and $Q4$ in equation (4.4) are dummy variables indicating whether the market area was in the highest or lowest expenditure quartile in 1990 and are intended to capture the effects of regression to the mean.

Table 4.7 presents estimation results. The models in columns 1 and 3 do not control for the initial level of expenditures; the models in columns 2 and 4 do. For Part A, the coefficients on the initial level of systemwide market share are statistically insignificant. However, growth in systemwide market share over time is associated with lower expenditure growth. With controls for initial expenditure levels included, 10-percentage-point increases in systemwide market share are associated with 4.3-percentage-point reductions in expenditure growth rates. At least in this context, changes in HMO activity are more important than the initial level in determining spending growth.

The story is reversed for Medicare HMO market share. Although the initial level of Medicare market share is not significant, the results imply that 10-percentage-point increases in Medicare market share are associated with 4.5-percentage-point increases in the spending growth rate. These results, like those presented above, suggest that selection and simultaneity bias effects may outweigh any Medicare-specific spillovers.

For Part B, the initial level of systemwide HMO market share is again insignificant, but increases in market share over time are associated with decreases in expenditure growth rates. With the controls for the initial level of spending included, a 10-percentage-point increase in systemwide market share would reduce the expenditure growth rate by 1.1 percentage points. Both the initial level of Medicare HMO market share and the 1990–94 change in Medicare market share are associated with decreases in expenditures. Ten-percentage-point increases in the initial market share level are associated with 2.0-percentage-point reductions in expenditure growth, and 10-percentage-point increases over time are associated with 2.8-percentage-point reductions, suggesting spillover effects directly associated with Medicare HMO market share may be strong enough to overcome positive effects of selection and simultaneity bias.

Table 4.7
Results from first-differenced models

Variables	Part A		Part B	
	No initial expenditure controls (1)	Include initial expenditure controls (2)	No initial expenditure controls (3)	Include initial expenditure controls (4)
1990 systemwide HMO market share /10	0.008 (0.006)	0.009 (0.005)	−0.003 (0.003)	−0.002 (0.003)
Δ Systemwide HMO market share	−0.043 (0.008)	−0.043 (0.008)	−0.013 (0.005)	−0.011 (0.005)
1990 Medicare HMO market share /10	−0.010 (0.006)	−0.006 (0.006)	−0.021 (0.004)	−0.020 (0.003)
Δ Medicare HMO market share	0.045 (0.013)	0.041 (0.013)	−0.027 (0.008)	−0.028 (0.007)
Highest quartile of 1990 expenditures	—	0.020 (0.034)	—	−0.043 (0.020)
Lowest quartile of 1990 expenditures	—	0.081 (0.036)	—	0.027 (0.021)
N	801	801	801	801
R^2	0.519	0.534	0.397	0.461

Note: Standard errors are in parentheses. The dependent variable is the 1990–94 difference in the natural logarithm of expenditures per beneficiary (the mean is 0.357 for Part A and 0.271 for Part B). Regressions also contain controls for 1990 levels and 1990–94 changes in area population demographics, physicians per capita, and hospital beds per capita. Regressions are weighted by 1990 Medicare enrollment.

V. Discussion

We draw two sets of conclusions from these results. First, increases in systemwide HMO market share reduce expenditures for the care of Medicare FFS beneficiaries, a population that should be well-insulated from the direct effects of managed care. Increases in systemwide market share from 10 to 20% were associated with decreases of 1.9 to 2.3% in Part A expenditures and 1.2 to 1.7% in Part B expenditures. This is consistent with the hypothesis that managed care can have significant spillover effects that broadly influence the entire health care system's structure and functioning.

Given Medicare's structure, we believe that these findings largely reflect spillover effects that occur through the availability and use of health care services. For example, Baker and Wheeler (1997) report that increases in HMO market share are associated with a decline in the systemwide availability of MRI equipment. Cutler and Sheiner (1997) also report that areas with high levels of HMO activity may have reduced technology availability. Reductions in the general availability of health care equipment and technologies may translate into reduced systemwide use, providing a mechanism for reductions in spending. Increases in HMO market share may also lead to changes in health care providers' behavior independent of any changes in the availability of services.

By extrapolation, these results believe that managed care may also influence the care provided to non–managed-care patients outside of Medicare. In fact, because the Medicare FFS program is not subject to the competition that pervades the non-Medicare sector of the health care market, and because spillover effects that occur through changes in price are not likely to be observed in Medicare data, spillover effects in other sectors of the health care market might even be larger.

From a policy standpoint, these results suggest that managed care's systemwide effects should be considered when assessing the ongoing shift toward managed care and that the interests of non–managed-care patients should be considered when policies that would influence managed-care growth are evaluated. In addition, scrutiny should be given to studies that examine differences between utilization and outcomes of managed-care and non–managed-care patients, because managed care may induce changes in these variables for non–managed-care patients as well.

Second, spillover effects associated directly with Medicare HMO market share are likely to be small. Updating previous work revealed that increases in Medicare HMO market share are associated with increases in Part A expenditures, the opposite of previous findings. Because the Medicare HMO market share coefficients capture the effects of selection bias as well as any spillover effects, these findings suggest that biased selection's expenditure-increasing effects are substantially larger than any expenditure-decreasing spillover effects.

Our more recent results may differ from previous results for a number of reasons. The importance of Medicare-specific spillovers for Part A expenditures may have diminished over time to the point where they are no longer a strong force. As a second possibility, selection bias may have become stronger over time. A third possibility stems from the relationship between Medicare and systemwide HMO market share. If Medicare market share was better correlated with systemwide HMO market share in the 1980s than in the 1990s, then the Medicare HMO market share coefficients in the earlier studies may have reflected systemwide spillover effects to a greater degree. In the presence of expenditure-reducing systemwide spillovers, this could have caused studies using Medicare market share to show an expenditure-decreasing effect in earlier years when in fact the real action was systemwide.

It is difficult to evaluate the relative strengths of these possible explanations, and further study of them will be necessary. We did explore the possibility that the correlation between Medicare and systemwide market share has changed over time. Because geographically detailed data on systemwide market shares are not available for the 1980s, we used state-level data to examine the correlation between the 1986–90 change in Medicare and systemwide market share, and compared it to the correlation between the 1990–94 changes in Medicare and systemwide market share. For the earlier time period, the correlation is 0.27, whereas for the latter time period, the correlation is 0.20. Although neither of these correlations is very high, they do leave open the possibility that some of the difference in the results is due to a reduction in the extent to which Medicare HMO market share proxies systemwide market share.

Regardless of the cause, these findings suggest that conclusions about Medicare-specific spillovers for Part A expenditures drawn from previous studies that used Medicare-specific HMO market share may substantially overstate actual spillovers. This finding does not prove that Medicare market share has no associated spillover effect, only that any spillover effect that is present is smaller than other expenditure-increasing effects associated with increasing Medicare market share (e.g., selection bias).

For Part B expenditures, we find evidence consistent with the presence of spillover effects that are associated with Medicare market share. But holding systemwide market share constant, the magnitude of these results is much smaller than the effect of Medicare market share observed in models that do not include systemwide market share. Our results imply that increases in market share may be associated with decreases in expenditures on the order of 1 to 2% after controlling for systemwide market share, whereas earlier models that did not control for systemwide market share reported results generally at least twice as large.

The existence of a spillover effect that stems directly from Medicare HMO market share is interesting, given the relative weakness of the financial incentives within Medicare. Learning spillovers or other phenomena may occur between physicians treating the elderly that are confined to the Medicare world. Further investigation of the source of this finding will be needed.

Taken broadly, these results suggest that managed care transforms the functioning of the entire health care system. But in the context of Medicare reform discussions, these results suggest that caution should be exercised before relying on spillover effects to generate savings from increases in Medicare HMO market share. Although our results do not rule out the possibility of spillovers directly associated with increasing Medicare market share, they suggest that the effect may be much smaller than has been previously thought. The presence of a systemwide spillover effect, to which changes in Medicare HMO market share could contribute, does suggest that Medicare HMO market share can have spillover effects but that the impact of a change in Medicare market share may be limited by the role of Medicare HMO activity within the broader scope of systemwide HMO activity.

Appendix A: Computing the Effect of a Change in Medicare HMO Market Share for Equation (4.2).

Let P_m and P_o denote the number of people in an area who are in Medicare and not in Medicare, respectively, and E_m and E_o denote

HMO enrollment among Medicare beneficiaries and the rest of the population, respectively. Then, we can write $M=(E_m/P_m)$ and $S=(E_m+E_o)/(P_m+P_o)$. The regression coefficients β_1 and β_2 capture part of the effect of increasing Medicare HMO market share. To separate out the effect of Medicare HMO market share, we write out the relevant parts of equation (4.2), inserting the enrollment and population variables:

$$\log(E_{i,t}) = \beta_1 \frac{E_m + E_o}{P_m + P_o} + \beta_2 \left(\frac{E_m + E_o}{P_m + P_o}\right)^2 + \beta_3 \frac{E_m}{P_m} + \beta_4 \left(\frac{E_m}{P_m}\right)^2.$$

This can be rewritten as:

$$\log(E_{i,t}) = \delta_1 \frac{E_m}{P_m} + \delta_2 \left(\frac{E_m}{P_m}\right)^2 + \beta_1 \frac{E_o}{P_m + P_o} + \beta_2 \left(\frac{E_o}{P_m + P_o}\right)^2.$$

where

$$\delta_1 = \frac{P_m}{P_m + P_o} \beta_1 + \beta_3$$

and

$$\delta_2 = \left(\frac{P_m}{P_m + P_o}\right)^2 \beta_2 + \beta_4.$$

That is, δ_1 and δ_2 determine the effect of an increase in Medicare market share, and they incorporate β_3 and β_4 along with scaled components reflecting the effects of systemwide market share β_1 and β_2, where the scaling factor is the proportion of the population in Medicare. In 1994, approximately 12.4% of the population was enrolled in Medicare, and the implementations of these formulas used in the paper use this value. Using δ_1 and δ_2 in place of β_3 and β_4, estimated percent changes in expenditures associated with given changes in Medicare HMO market share can be obtained using equation (4.3) in the text.

References

Baker, L. C. 1997. "The Effect of HMOs on Fee-for-Service Health Care Expenditures: Evidence from Medicare." *Journal of Health Economics* 16:453–82.

Baker, L. C. 1995. "County-Level Measures of HMO Enrollment and Market share." Stanford University, Stanford, CA. Mimeographed.

Baker, L. C. 1994. "Does Competition from HMOs Affect Fee-for-Service Physicians?" Working paper no. 4920, National Bureau of Economic Research, Cambridge, MA.

Baker, L. C., and M. L. Brown. 1997. "The Effect of Managed Care on Health Care Providers: Evidence from Mammography." Working paper no. 5987, National Bureau of Economic Research, Cambridge, MA.

Baker, L. C., and K. S. Corts. 1996. "HMO Penetration and the Cost of Health Care: Market Discipline or Market Segmentation?" *American Economic Review* 86:390–4.

Baker, L. C., and S. W. Wheeler. 1997. "HMOs and the Availability and Use of Magnetic Resonance Imaging." Stanford University, Stanford, CA. Manuscript.

Bergsten, C. D., and S. E. Palsbo. 1993. *HMO Market Penetration in the 54 Largest Metropolitan Statistical Areas, 1991.* Washington, DC: Group Health Association of America, April.

Chernew, M. 1995. "The Impact of Non-IPA HMOs on the Number of Hospitals and Hospital Capacity." *Inquiry* 32:143–54.

Clement, D. G., P. M. Gleason, and R. S. Brown. 1992. *The Effects of Risk Contract HMO Market Penetration on Medicare Fee-for-Service Costs.* Final report prepared for the Health Care Financing Administration, U.S. Department of Health and Human Services, Washington, DC, by Williamson Institute for Health Studies, Department of Health Administration, Medical College of Virginia, Richmond, VA, and Mathematica Policy Research, Princeton, NJ.

Cromwell, J., and J. B. Mitchell. 1986. "Physician-Induced Demand for Surgery." *Journal of Health Economics* 5:293–313.

Cutler, D. M., and L. Sheiner. 1997. "Managed Care and the Growth of Medical Expenditures." Harvard University, Cambridge, MA. Manuscript.

Dowd, B. E. 1987. "HMOs and Twin Cities Admission Rates." *Health Services Research* 21 (part I):177–88.

Feldman, R., B. E. Dowd, D. McCann, and A. Johnson. 1986. "The Competitive Impact of Health Maintenance Organizations on Hospital Finances: An Exploratory Study." *Journal of Health Politics, Policy, and Law* 10:675:98.

Frank, R. G., and W. P. Welch. 1985. "The Competitive Effects of HMOs: A Review of the Evidence." *Inquiry* 22:148–61.

Goldberg, L. G., and W. Greenberg. 1981. "The Determinants of HMO Enrollment and Growth." *Health Services Research* 16:421–38.

Goldberg, L. G., and W. Greenberg. 1979. "The Competitive Response of Blue Cross and Blue Shield to the Growth of Health Maintenance Organizations in Northern California and Hawaii." *Medical Care* 17:1019–28.

Group Health Association of America. 1990–1995, annually. *National Directory of HMOs.* Washington, DC: GHAA.

Hammonds, K. H. 1997. "Medicare Gets an Umbrella for an Avalanche." *Business Week*, 2 June, p. 44.

Hellinger, F. J. 1995. "Selection Bias in HMOs and PPOs: A Review of the Evidence." *Inquiry* 32:135–42.

Hellinger, F. J. 1987. "Selection Bias in Health Maintenance Organizations: Analysis of Recent Evidence." Health Care Financing Review 9:55–63.

Hill, J. W., and R. S. Brown. 1990. *Biased Selection in the TEFRA HMO/CMP Program.* Report prepared for the U.S. Department of Health and Human Services, Health Care Financing Administration, Baltimore, MD, by Mathematica Policy Research, Princeton, NJ. Contract no. 500-88-0006.

Interstudy. *Competitive Edge.* Excelsior, MN: Interstudy.

Luft, H. S., and R. H. Miller. 1988. "Patient Selection in a Competitive Health Care System." *Health Affairs* 7:97–111.

Luft, H. S., S. C. Maerki, and J. B. Travner 1986. "The competitive effects of health maintenance organizations: Another look at the evidence from Hawaii, Rochester, and Minneapolis/St. Paul," *Journal of Health Politics, Policy, and Law* 10:625–658.

Makuc, D. M., B. Haglund, D. D. Ingram, J. C. Kleinman, and J. J. Feldman. 1991. *Vital and Health Statistics—Health Care Service Areas for the United States.* Washington, DC: National Center for Health Statistics.

McClellan, M. B. 1997. "Hospital Reimbursement Incentives: An Empirical Analysis." *Journal of Economics and Management Strategy* 6:91–128.

McLaughlin, C. G. 1988. "The effect of HMOs on overall hospital expenses: Is Anything Left after Correcting for Simultaneity and Selectivity?" *Health Services Research* 23:421–41.

McLaughlin, C. G. 1987. HMO Growth and Hospital Expenses and Use: A Simultaneous-Equation Approach. Health Services Research 22:183–205.

Mitchell, J. B., G. Wedig, and J. Cromwell. 1989. "The Medicare Physician Fee Freeze: What Really Happened?" *Health Affairs* 8:21–33.

Noether, M. 1988. "Competition Among Hospitals." *Journal of Health Economics* 7:259–84.

Phelps, C. 1992. "Diffusion of information in medical care." *Journal of Economic Perspectives* 6:23–42.

Porell, F. W., and S. S. Wallack. 1990. "Medicare Risk Contracting: Determinants of Market Entry." Health Care Financing Review 12:75–85.

Robinson, J. C. 1996. "Decline in Hospital Utilization and Cost Inflation under Managed Care in California." *Journal of the American Medical Association* 276(13):1060–4.

Robinson, J. C. 1991. "HMO Market Penetration and Hospital Cost Inflation in California." *Journal of the American Medical Association* 266:2719–23.

Rodgers, J., and K. E. Smith. 1995. *Do Medicare HMOs reduce fee-for-service costs?* Health Policy Economics Group report. Washington DC: Price Waterhouse LLP.

Welch, W. P. 1994. "HMO Market Share and Its Effect on Local Medicare Costs. In *HMOs and the Elderly,* ed. H. S. Luft, 231–49. Ann Arbor, MI: Health Administration Press.

5

Persistence of Medicare Expenditures among Elderly Beneficiaries

Alan M. Garber, *Veterans Affairs Palo Alto Health Care System, Stanford University, National Bureau of Economic Research, Inc.*
Thomas E. MaCurdy, *Stanford University, National Bureau of Economic Research, Inc.*
Mark B. McClellan, *Stanford University, National Bureau of Economic Research, Inc.*

Executive Summary

The highly uneven distribution of Medicare payments among elderly beneficiaries, combined with the predictability of some of the expenditures, poses several challenges to the Medicare program. We present information about the distribution of Medicare expenditures among beneficiaries in specific years, accompanied by new evidence on the extent to which Medicare payments for the care of individual beneficiaries persist over long time periods. Our analysis is based on a longitudinal population of Medicare enrollees during the years 1987 to 1995. We find that high-cost users accounted for a disproportionate share of the growth of Medicare Part A (hospital) payments during this period, but that an increase in the number of beneficiaries using covered services was largely responsible for the growth of Medicare Part B payments. Few beneficiaries are in the highest-cost categories for multiple years; the high mortality rates of individuals who use medical services heavily, whether the expenditures occur in one year or repeatedly, limits the extent of expenditure persistence. Even among survivors, it is unusual to remain in the highest-cost categories for multiple years. Nevertheless, individuals with high expenditures in one year are likely to have higher than average expenditures in other years, and expenditures are highly skewed even over a period of nine years. Any policy to reform Medicare will need to accommodate expenditure persistence to provide adequate coverage for all beneficiaries.

I. Introduction

Policy debates about controlling health care costs and about the value of medical expenditures necessarily focus on the minority of individuals who incur high costs. These debates are particularly pressing for

This work was supported in part by the Commonwealth Fund, the National Institute on Aging, and the Olin Foundation. We are grateful for the assistance of Hoon Byun, Jean-Paul Sursock, and John Johnson.

the Medicare program for several reasons. First, because it covers the elderly and individuals with long-term disabilities, Medicare has a disproportionate share of high-cost users of health care: Even though Medicare covers only one-sixth of the population, those covered account for around one-third of U.S. health care expenditures. Second, Medicare is an enormous entitlement program whose expenditures have been rising rapidly. Substantial reform of the program appears inevitable: According to current projections of the Medicare trustees, the Medicare Part A trust fund will become insolvent by 2001. Although the Medicare recipients we study are somewhat homogeneous because all are elderly, even within this population expenditures are highly skewed. In 1994, for example, 62% of Medicare beneficiaries had reimbursements averaging less than $1,000, whereas 4% had claims of $25,000 or more, and an additional 4% had reimbursements of between $15,000 and $25,000 (Gornick et al. 1996). Every year, approximately 10% of Medicare beneficiaries account for three-fourths of program outlays; health expenditures in the general population are similarly skewed (Berk and Monheit 1992). Judgments about some of the most difficult issues for Medicare reform involve the persistence of expenditures for this subset of beneficiaries.

Considerable empirical research, along with the prevalence of chronic health problems in the Medicare population, suggest that an individual's past use of medical services helps predict future use. The 46% of the general population that has at least one chronic condition generates about three-quarters of all health expenditures; about 88% of Americans 65 and older have at least one chronic condition (Hoffman, Rice, and Sung 1996). Not all chronic conditions are serious enough to require extensive, ongoing medical treatment. But once a person has been treated for end-stage renal disease, severe congestive heart failure, cancer, emphysema, or many other serious conditions, we know that he or she is likely to use medical care more frequently and incur higher costs than individuals without a serious chronic illness. For similar reasons, a man or woman who has high medical expenditures in one year is likely to generate significantly higher than average health expenditures in future years. This does not mean that it is possible to predict any single person's health expenditures with precision, but it does imply that entire classes of people can be identified as potentially high-cost patients on the basis of such characteristics as their age, sex, race, and medical diagnoses as well as their prior treatments and expenditure history. Even though these features are associated with substantial predictable differences in expenditures, however, the individuals involved often know more than insurers or health care providers about their likelihood of experiencing high costs. It is difficult to capture all of the subtle factors that may influence use of medical care in even detailed databases, and some uses of medical care by individuals—such as elective surgical procedures in previously healthy beneficiaries—may be expected yet not predictable on the basis of any characteristics that a payor or an analyst can observe.

These distinctive features of health care use combine to create some very difficult and complex policy problems for Medicare, with contradictory solutions. The fact that health involves small risks of potentially serious and costly diseases implies that individuals ordinarily want to obtain some kind of insurance against the possibility of these adverse events. Insurance works best when its potential purchasers have no special information about their risk of an adverse event and when they all face similar risks—whether the risk of loss involves a fire, an automobile accident, a flood, or a health problem. If risks differ, and if the potential purchaser knows more about his or her risk than the insurer, then risk selection is likely to create problems for insurance markets (Pauly 1986). At any price, an insurance plan appears to be a better value for someone who expects to use a lot of medical care than for someone who does not plan to use much care. If each health plan can charge only one price to enrollees, and if different kinds of health plans are available, individuals may end up with too little insurance. Lower-risk individuals may buy less generous insurance than they would prefer to avoid plans with higher-risk enrollees (Rothschild and Stiglitz 1976). This phenomenon may even cause "death spirals" of unstable premium growth in the most generous insurance plan choices (Price and Mays 1985).

One solution to this problem is to restrict plan choice: If everyone must join a single plan, there is little potential for risk segmentation. Indeed, when nearly all Medicare beneficiaries belonged to "traditional" Medicare, risk selection was not an issue. Although restricting choice limits the adverse selection problem, many critics have argued that it creates other serious problems. With a captive audience, an insurer does not need to make sure that it is producing the benefits and services that its enrollees most desire for the cost. Enrollees also have little incentive to consider whether the services they receive in the plan are worth the expenditures involved. For these reasons, Alain Enthoven (Enthoven and Singer 1996) and others have advocated reforms that increase health plan choice and thus competition to increase efficiency in Medicare. Among other things, such reforms would give individuals more alternative plans (and more useful information about those choices) and stronger financial incentives to choose a plan that is worth the cost. For example, Medicare might pay a fixed amount per year toward a beneficiary's purchase of any of a range of accepted plans. But such reforms could increase pressures for adverse selection and substantially increase many beneficiaries' out-of-pocket costs of care. Healthy beneficiaries would have stronger incentives to select less generous plans, and individuals with chronic illnesses might have to pay considerably more for plans that provided better coverage for their conditions. The system of plan choice that Medicare uses today may have developed in part to avoid such problems. Beneficiaries can choose to join managed-care plans, but in contrast to the choice system used by many private firms, price competition among such plans is severely limited. As a result, plans must compete largely on the basis of benefits, which limits one of the dimensions on which selection can occur (McClellan 1997).

One approach to address the adverse selection problem while allowing health plan choice is to risk adjust the premiums that health insurers and health plans receive. Improving risk adjustment methods has become a major research and policy concern (Iezzoni 1994). A principal goal of risk adjustment methods is to compensate health plans and providers for the intrinsically higher costs of care associated with higher-risk enrollees and conversely to limit the financial rewards from attracting relatively healthy enrollees. A perfect risk adjustment system would feature premiums that matched an individual enrollee's risk, so that health plans and providers would compete on the basis of quality of care rather than risk selection.

Risk adjustment, however, is not currently able to overcome adverse selection and the problems it causes. First, perfect risk adjustment is not feasible. State-of-the-art risk adjustment methods based on diagnoses typically explain about 7% of the variation in medical expenditures from one year to the next. Although much of the remaining 93% may not be predictable, and thus is not a problem for insurance markets, a considerable fraction of it is likely to be predictable, in the sense that beneficiaries know it when they are choosing plans. For example, many intensive medical procedures such as elective joint replacements or cataract operations are largely predictable, in that an enrollee may be able to wait several months from the time that he or she suspects that the operation would be beneficial, so that the need for the procedure is known well in advance. In addition, prior use of intensive procedures such as hospitalizations or major operations, as well as prior expenditures, have considerably more predictive power for explaining expenditures compared to diagnoses alone. But if intensive treatments and prior expenditures are included in risk adjustment methods, they introduce another incentive problem: An individual or a plan would be more willing to provide higher-cost treatments, because they would know that providing those treatments today would increase the payments they would receive in the future.[1]

Finally, risk adjustment may have substantial distributional implications, which many economists have argued should be addressed directly, or at least should be understood explicitly when they are undertaken implicitly in social programs. To the extent that expenditure differences in the future are known and Medicare compensates beneficiaries for these differences, then Medicare is redistributing wealth from low- to high-risk individuals rather than simply providing insurance. For example, if I know that I am likely to develop chronic lung disease, because it runs in my family or because I smoke, it might make sense for me to save money now in anticipation of the costs of hospitalization or higher costs of my insurance in the future. Such precautionary saving is expected when future events are certain and compensation through an insurance program is not available. Without risk adjustment, I might save more, because I would not expect as much compensation from Medicare over my lifetime; with risk adjustment, I would probably be better off, but those with lower risks of chronic illnesses—who would presumably receive fewer benefits or would contribute to the risk adjustment payments—might be worse off. Every policy option for Medicare has distributional implications for those with and without high risk of illness, and the potential magnitudes of predictable differences in health costs across individuals imply that such redistribution may be large.

This review of some of the conflicting efficiency and distributional problems facing potential reforms in the Medicare program highlights our surprisingly limited understanding of a crucial topic for balancing all of these concerns: the persistence of expenditures for Medicare beneficiaries over long time periods. Virtually all the studies of risk adjustment and adverse selection in Medicare assess differences in risk

---

1. This is another form of the moral hazard problem.

from one year to the next—a relatively brief portion of most beneficiaries' years enrolled in Medicare. This limited perspective can lead to a correspondingly limited and potentially misleading perspective on Medicare reforms. For example, the presence of a chronic illness such as cancer in one year may predict expenditures much higher than average in the next year, as the patient receives followup therapies to consolidate the initial cancer treatment. But if the cancer goes into remission or is cured, then the patient's expenditures may not be very much higher than average in subsequent years. Alternatively, an individual with very high expenditures due to a severe chronic illness such as advanced heart failure may die within several years of developing the condition, again limiting the illness's importance from the standpoint of long-term risk selection. The fact that 27% of Medicare expenditures occur in the last year of life suggests that this limitation on long-term persistence is important. Consequently, single-year expenditures or expenditure persistence over two years may give a misleading picture of longer-term expenditure persistence in Medicare; beneficiaries who have the highest expenditures over many years may look quite different from beneficiaries who have high expenditures over only two or three years. Thus policies based on year-to-year persistence may have unintended effects. They may target efforts to provide long-term access to adequate insurance and compensation on individuals who experience high-cost episodes of care for a year or two, rather than those who face the greatest problems of long-term expenditure persistence.

Another important reason to assess differences in Medicare expenditures over longer time periods concerns the "moving target" nature of Medicare policy problems. Treatments available for health problems change, with potentially important consequences for the concentration of expenditures and their persistence over time. For example, as new but costly treatments for irregular heart rhythms and heart failure become available, persistence may increase if individuals who would have died from the condition now survive longer with a costly chronic illness. If changes in treatment affect low- and high-cost patients differently, the concentration of expenditures in Medicare in 1992—and the reasons for the concentration—may be quite different from the concentration in 1997. Thus risk adjustment methods may become outdated as novel treatments are introduced, but there is little information with which to assess the performance of specific risk adjustment methods over time.

Moreover, to the extent that Medicare expenditure growth is a policy concern, understanding the sources of expenditure growth is critically important. Although a small fraction of individuals may account for a large share of expenditures at a given point in time, they may account for a relatively larger or smaller share of expenditure growth, suggesting that efforts to address expenditure growth should be adjusted accordingly.

For all of these reasons, a longer-term perspective on expenditure persistence can provide crucial evidence for policy. We present new evidence on the extent to which expenditures persist over long time periods in the Medicare program and on the contribution of high-cost beneficiaries to Medicare expenditure growth. Our analysis of persistently high medical expenditures is based on a longitudinal population of Medicare enrollees. The sample is representative of all Americans 65 years of age and older. We focus on the persistence of expenditures for services the Medicare program covers. However, we also consider these beneficiaries' out-of-pocket payments and thus total expenditures for Medicare-covered services. Certain medical expenditures not covered by Medicare, in particular outpatient pharmaceuticals and long-term nursing home stays, are not included.

In the next section, we describe our data set in more detail. The section after that presents results on expenditure persistence over long time periods. We review the concentration of expenditure growth in high-cost users leading to significant increases in the skewness of Medicare expenditures over time. We also describe in detail how expenditures persist over time periods as long as a decade and analyze the contribution of death and returns to lower expenditure levels in limiting long-term persistence. We find that expenditure persistence over long time periods is actually quite different from that suggested by year-to-year persistence. In the final section, we discuss some implications of these results for a range of proposed Medicare policy reforms and highlight some further questions for research.

II. Data

To study expenditure persistence, we compiled longitudinal summary data from all Medicare claims filed by a random sample of approximately 37,000 beneficiaries (0.08% of all Medicare beneficiaries) over the nine-year period from 1987 through 1995. We focused on total Medicare expenditures and their major components: Part A hospital expenditures (including both acute and nonacute admissions covered by Medicare), hospice expenditures (Part A), home health expenditures (mainly Part A), outpatient hospital expenditures (Part B), and physician and other supplier expenditures (Part B).[2] We considered two principal measures of each of these types of expenditures: actual Medicare program expenditures (Medicare reimbursement) for the care of beneficiaries and total expenditures for these services, inclusive of patient payments. Thus total expenditures included the beneficiary's liabilities due to copayments, deductibles, and maximum limits for Medicare payments. Expenditures for services Medicaid does not cover at all, such as outpatient prescription drugs, were not included.[3] For the most part, beneficiary payments track Medicare reimbursements closely. Although we focus primarily on Medicare program payments in the results below, results for total reimbursement and patient payments were quite similar.

We calculated annual expenditures by summing up all valid claims of each type. We excluded all beneficiaries younger than 65 years of age as well as beneficiaries who resided outside the United States or were enrolled in health maintenance organizations.[4] We converted all costs into constant 1996 dollars using the general Consumer Price Index (CPI).

III. Results

Contribution of High-Cost Beneficiaries to Expenditure Growth

Early in the 1980s, the Health Care Financing Administration addressed rising hospital costs by introducing the Prospective Payment System (PPS) for Medicare-financed hospital care covered by Part A.

---

2. We integrated information from the five major administrative data files the Health Care Financing Administration maintains: claims for hospital and skilled nursing facility stays (MEDPAR, or Medical Provider Analysis and Review files), home health care (HHA, or Home Health Agency), hospice care, and outpatient visits and other Part B services (from the "Outpatient 5% Bill Skeleton File" and BMAD, or the Part B Medicare Annual Data files).

3. The other major type of uncovered service is long-term stays in nursing homes. Nursing home admissions after an acute-care admission are covered for the first 100 days, so that Medicare now covers the vast majority of shorter, nonacute hospital stays for the elderly.

4. We excluded these patients because detailed claims information—which we intend to use in later work—is not reliably available for them. Assigning the relevant Medicare Annual Adjusted Per Capita Cost (AAPCC) rate for the HMO beneficiaries and including them in the analysis does not appreciably alter our results.

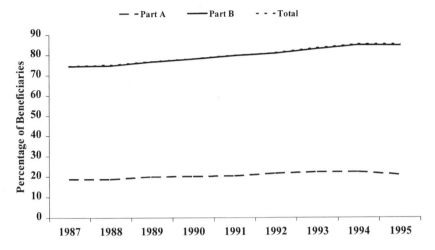

Figure 5.1
Percentage of beneficiaries who receive Part A and Part B services

Subsequently, it introduced changes in payments for Part B (primarily physician) services as well, although none represented as dramatic a change in the basic payment approach as the introduction of PPS. By the late 1980s and early 1990s, Part B drew more attention because its expenditures were rising. Although Part B claims are usually much smaller than Part A claims, many more Medicare recipients have Part B claims. As figure 5.1 shows, essentially all Medicare recipients who have any claim in a given year will have at least one Part B claim. Any other result would be surprising, because it is difficult to be hospitalized (largely reimbursed by Part A) without receiving the services of a physician (reimbursed by Part B). In addition, the fraction of Medicare recipients using Part B services has traditionally been large and grew substantially from 1987, when the fraction was 74%, to 1995, when 84% had claims.

An immediately apparent group of "high-cost users" of Medicare-covered services consists of all beneficiaries who were hospitalized, that is, who had a Part A claim. Between 1987 and 1993, the fraction using Part A services grew slowly, from 19% to 22%, and actually declined to 21% in 1995. Despite the slow growth and late decline in the fraction with hospital claims, inflation-adjusted Part A expenditures among hospitalized patients grew more rapidly than the Part B claims among those who used Part B services. Real Part A reimbursements per individual with a Part A claim rose by 58% between 1987

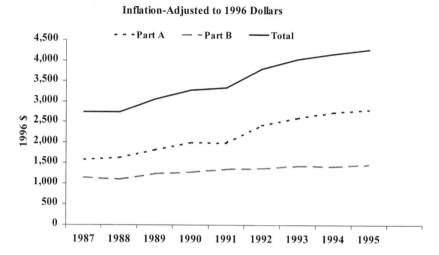

Figure 5.2
Average Medicare payments per elderly beneficiary, 1987–1995

and 1995, while reimbursements for Part B patients with claims rose by only 12%. Overall Medicare reimbursements for patients receiving services rose by 37%. Thus, in a period when Medicare's PPS for hospital care had been in place and when hospital use generally declined, the cost of each hospital admission, rather than growth in the fraction with hospital claims, drove Part A expenditure growth. In contrast, the number using services, rather than the total value of claims per recipient using services, explained most of the growth in Part B expenditures.

As can be seen in figure 5.2, combined Part A and Part B expenditures per Medicare beneficiary rose substantially from 1987 to 1995. In 1996 constant dollars, expenditures per enrollee were $2,736 (of which $1,153 was Part B) in 1987 and $4,267 ($1,471 Part B) in 1995, a 56% increase. The beneficiaries who had Part A claims used Part B–reimbursed services more than twice as heavily as average Medicare beneficiaries. These services include both office visits and physician services administered during hospitalization.

During this period expenditure growth was concentrated among the high-cost users of Medicare-reimbursed services (figure 5.3). Although few Medicare enrollees had no claims (about a quarter in 1987, and only 15% in 1995), the typical enrollee's claims were modest. Median expenditures rose from $647 in 1987 to $884 in 1995, a 37% cumulative rate of growth. The group with the top 2% of expenditures, however,

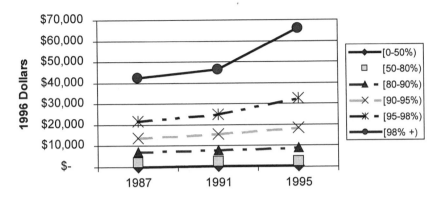

Figure 5.3
Average combined Part A and Part B Medicare expenditures by percentile groups in selected years

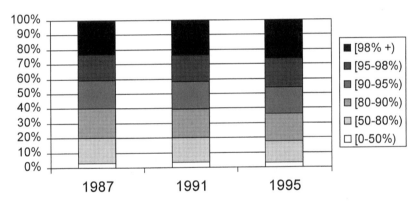

Figure 5.4
Shares of combined Part A and Part B Medicare expenditures by percentile groups in selected years

experienced a cumulative rate of growth of 52%, as average expenditures rose from $28,000 in 1987 to $42,000 in 1995. Changes in the share of expenditures attributable to each percentile group also reflected this concentration of growth in the upper percentiles of expenditures, as figure 5.4 shows. This figure plots the proportion of combined Part A and Part B expenditures due to each percentile group by expenditure and shows that by 1995 the top 2% of Medicare recipients, ranked by expenditure levels, accounted for about the same fraction of overall expenditures as the lower 90%. The percentage of expenditures falling into the very highest percentiles, not shown in figure 5.4, suggests an even more dramatic concentration of expenditures among the highest cost users. In 1995, the group falling between the 99th and 99.5th percentile accounted for 7% of all expenditures, the group from 99.5th to 99.9th percentile accounted for an additional 8%, and the top one-tenth of one percent of recipients accounted for nearly 4% of Medicare expenditures. Overall, therefore, the top 1% accounted for about 19% of Medicare expenditures; the portion of expenditures attributable to the highest percentiles tended to rise with time.

The upper percentiles were also responsible for a rising share of Part A expenditures. The 80th percentile is a particularly interesting group because this very crudely approximates the percentile that would result from having a hospitalization during the calendar year. The 80th–90th percentile group's share of total expenditures declined slightly, from about 20% to 18%, between 1987 and 1995. Although average Medicare expenditures for this group rose by 15% over these years, average expenditures for the 95th percentile rose by 39%, and average expenditures for the 98th percentile rose by 52%. Thus high-cost users of Medicare services were disproportionately responsible for both the level and the rate of growth of Medicare expenditures.

Persistence of Expenditures over Multiple Years

Skewness in annual expenditures, even if it increases over time, does not imply that the adverse selection problems noted in the introduction will occur. Such problems occur only if variation in expenditures is predictable. One aspect of predictability is persistence: Do Medicare beneficiaries with high expenditures in one year tend to have high expenditures subsequently? The answer, according to the results in tables 5.1a to 5.1d, is yes. Each of these tables presents information about beneficiaries according to their expenditure group in 1989 (top set of rows) and 1993. Figures 5.5a (for 1989) and 5.5b (for 1993) illustrate graphically some of the findings from table 5.1a. Figure 5.5a shows that if a beneficiary was in a high expenditure group in 1989, his or her expenditures one or two years before, or one or two years later, were expected to be higher than average. Similarly, a person in the low expenditure group in 1989 could be expected to have lower than average expenditures in the years immediately preceding or following 1989. Figure 5.5b demonstrates that these results also apply to 1993 categories and are especially pronounced for the top percentiles. In both 1987 and 1991, for example, the mean expenditures for

Table 5.1a
Persistence of expenditures for beneficiaries in various expenditure categories (average Medicare expenditures over time for surviving persons in category, in 1996$)

Expenditure category	Year								
	1987	1988	1989	1990	1991	1992	1993	1994	1995
Beneficiary rank in 1989									
Low (0–50th percentile)	1,233	1,076	165	1,969	2,352	—	—	—	—
Middle (50th–95th percentile)	3,322	3,712	4,771	5,244	5,418	—	—	—	—
50th–80th percentile	2,998	3,167	2,235	4,474	4,909	—	—	—	—
80th–95th percentile	3,955	4,786	9,846	6,993	6,658	—	—	—	—
High (95th+ percentile)	5,139	8,343	34,015	13,132	9,539	—	—	—	—
Beneficiary rank in 1993									
Low (0–50th percentile)	—	—	—	—	1,416	1,352	211	2,364	2,896
Middle (50th–95th percentile)	—	—	—	—	3,880	5,186	5,758	6,280	6,536
50th–80th percentile	—	—	—	—	3,321	4,055	2,509	4,926	5,628
80th–95th percentile	—	—	—	—	4,978	7,428	12,256	9,399	8,829
High (95th+ percentile)	—	—	—	—	6,965	11,627	41,921	16,164	13,636

Table 5.1b
Persistence of expenditures for beneficiaries in various expenditure categories (average Medicare expenditures over time for survivors and decedents in category, in 1996$)

Expenditure category	Year								
	1987	1988	1989	1990	1991	1992	1993	1994	1995
Beneficiary rank in 1989									
Low (0–50th percentile)	1,233	1,076	165	1,932	2,238	—	—	—	—
Middle (50th–95th percentile)	3,322	3,712	4,771	4,817	4,633	—	—	—	—
50th–80th percentile	2,998	3,167	2,235	4,283	4,464	—	—	—	—
80th–95th percentile	3,955	4,786	9,846	5,884	4,969	—	—	—	—
High (95th + percentile)	5,139	8,343	34,015	9,439	5,501	—	—	—	—
Beneficiary rank in 1993									
Low (0–50th percentile)	—	—	—	—	1,416	1,352	211	2,322	2,752
Middle (50th–95th percentile)	—	—	—	—	3,880	5,186	5,758	5,740	5,477
50th–80th percentile	—	—	—	—	3,321	4,055	2,509	4,718	5,087
80th–95th percentile	—	—	—	—	4,978	7,428	12,256	7,775	6,247
High (95th + percentile)	—	—	—	—	6,965	11,627	41,921	12,441	8,320

Table 5.1c
Cumulative percentage of beneficiaries in various expenditure categories who die in subsequent years

Expenditure category	Year								
	1987	1988	1989	1990	1991	1992	1993	1994	1995
Beneficiary rank in 1989									
Low (0–50th percentile)	—	—	1.9	4.9	8.4	12.2	16.5	20.8	25.0
Middle (50th–95th percentile)	—	—	8.1	14.5	21.2	27.1	32.7	38.1	43.1
50th–80th percentile	—	—	4.2	9.0	15.2	20.2	25.5	31.0	35.9
80th–95th percentile	—	—	15.8	25.3	33.2	40.8	47.0	52.3	57.5
High (95th+ percentile)	—	—	28.0	42.1	48.8	55.8	61.0	64.7	68.9
Beneficiary rank in 1993									
Low (0–50th percentile)	—	—	—	—	—	—	1.7	4.7	8.0
Middle (50th–95th percentile)	—	—	—	—	—	—	8.5	15.6	22.4
50th–80th percentile	—	—	—	—	—	—	4.2	9.2	15.4
80th–95th percentile	—	—	—	—	—	—	17.0	28.3	36.3
High (95th+ percentile)	—	—	—	—	—	—	22.6	37.7	49.2

Table 5.1d
Persistence of expenditures for beneficiaries in various expenditure categories (percentage of beneficiaries occupying particular categories)

	Year																
	Two years before				One year before				Current year	One year after				Two years after			
Expenditure category	H*	M	L	D	H	M	L	D		H	M	L	D	H	M	L	D
Beneficiary rank in 1989																	
Low (0–50th percentile)	1.2	21.1	77.7		1.0	19.9	79.2		L	2.1	23.9	72.1	1.9	2.5	27.0	65.7	4.9
Middle (50th–95th percentile)	4.2	46.7	49.1		4.9	51.8	43.2		M	5.7	52.1	34.1	8.2	5.9	46.6	33.0	14.6
High (95th+ percentile)	8.1	49.6	42.3		14.4	57.1	28.6		H	15.2	43.5	13.1	28.2	8.8	34.2	14.5	42.5
Beneficiary rank in 1993																	
Low (0–50th percentile)	1.2	22.4	76.4		0.8	21.4	77.8		L	2.1	24.8	71.3	1.8	2.5	28.4	64.1	5.0
Middle (50th–95th percentile)	4.3	49.3	46.4		5.4	53.7	40.9		M	5.7	54.4	31.2	8.7	5.6	46.8	31.2	16.4
High (95th+ percentile)	10.2	53.7	36.1		18.0	54.8	27.1		H	17.9	47.5	11.5	23.0	10.5	36.0	14.4	39.2

*H = high expenditure (95th+ percentile); D = dead; L = low expenditure (0–50th percentile); M = middle expenditure (50th–95th percentile).

the group that fell between the 50th and 80th percentiles in 1989 were more than double those of the low-ranking group from 1989. As expected when expenditures are moderately persistent, although high (low) expenditures in 1989 are associated with high (low) expenditures in the years before and after, the variation in expenditures by percentile group is greatest during 1989. This observation merely reflects the fact that the percentile groups are based on 1989 expenditures, not that the overall skewness in expenditures was different in the other years. It is consistent with simple regression to the mean.

These results, which also appear in table 5.1a, are calculated by assuming that decedents are no longer considered part of the population generating costs. Thus, after they die they are not included in the denominator (i.e., population size) used to calculate average expenditures. For most purposes, this is the most appropriate way to view decedents. However, in other circumstances one might want to consider decedents part of the relevant population even after they die. Suppose that health insurance contracts are written for three years, so that premiums are paid at the outset to provide coverage for the entire three years. In effect, a person who dies during the first year continues to be part of the relevant population and has contributed to insurer revenues for the entire three years but is certain to generate no further costs after death. From this perspective, from the time of death a decedent is the same as a survivor with zero medical expenses. Table 5.1b presents results like those of table 5.1a, except that decedents continue to be treated as part of the population and are assigned zero expenditures after death. Figure 5.6 displays these results graphically as they apply to the 1993 base year. As expected, inclusion of decedents reduces the amount of apparent persistence; in the years following 1989 and 1993, the high-group average expenditures are not as high as when only survivors are included. The approach of death is associated with high expenditures, but death itself blunts the persistence of high expenditures.

Since decedents have disproportionately high costs, high-cost users must have relatively high mortality rates. Figure 5.7 (and table 5.1c) show that mortality rates are relatively high for Medicare recipients in the top percentiles of expenditures and that the excess mortality is concentrated in the first years after the high expenditures. Cumulative mortality during the succeeding two years is about three times as high for those in the high-expenditure group as for those in the low-expenditure group. The excess mortality is particularly great during

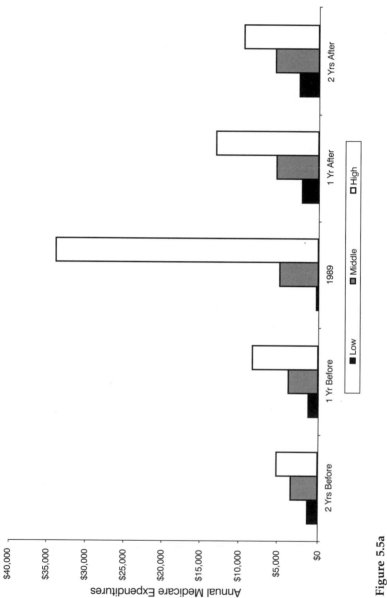

Figure 5.5a
Average expenditures over time for beneficiaries in the low (0–50th percentile), middle (50–95th percentile), and high (95%+ percentile) expenditure categories in 1989

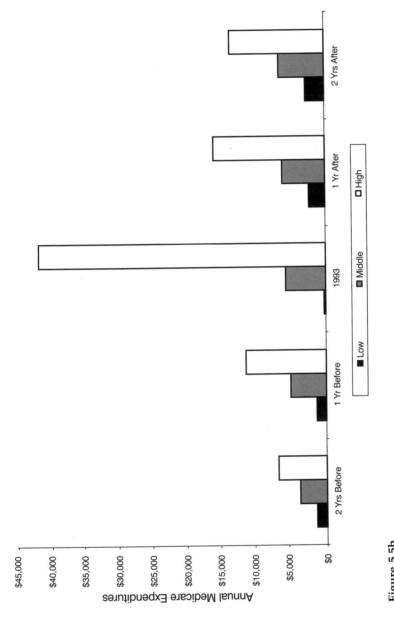

Figure 5.5b
Average expenditures over time for beneficiaries in the low, middle, and high expenditure categories in 1993

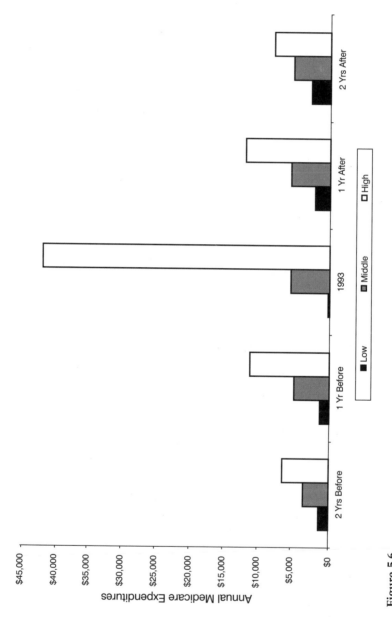

Figure 5.6
Average expenditures over time for beneficiaries in the low, middle, and high expenditure categories in 1993, decedents included

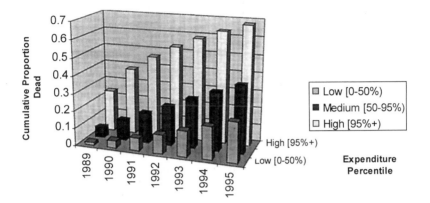

Figure 5.7
Cumulative death rates of the 1989 expenditure groups

the year of high expenditures; for example, during 1989, the highest percentile group had more than 14 times the mortality rate of the lower half of the Medicare beneficiaries. Although the dramatic difference in mortality rates narrows over time, in every subsequent year the annual mortality rate of the beneficiary group that had high expenditures in 1989 equals or exceeds that of the group that had low expenditures in 1989. A similar phenomenon can be seen in the lower panel of the table, which gives results by 1993 expenditure rank. Mortality rates increase with the expenditure level, even several years after the high expenditures are incurred.

Perhaps the simplest view of persistence of expenditures across years appears in table 5.1d, which shows the rank group in various years according to the rank group in either 1989 or 1993. For example, about 78% of the beneficiaries who were in the low-expenditure group in 1989 had been in the low-expenditure group two years before, and about 66% of them remained in the low group two years after. Of the beneficiaries in the high-expenditure group in 1989, only 42% had been in the low group two years before, and only 43% were in the low group two years later. The general pattern of persistence was the same for the 1993 groups. Note that high-expenditure individuals are more likely to be in the high-expenditure group than either the middle or the low groups, either two years before or two years after the baseline year of 1989 or 1993. But the 40% mortality rate within two years of being in the high-expenditure group necessarily limits the persistence of high expenditures.

Expenditures for the care of Medicare beneficiaries, according to these results, are neither highly persistent nor uncorrelated from one year to the next. Beneficiaries who have high expenditures in one year are likely to have high expenditures the next year and in subsequent years and are likely to have had higher expenditures in the past. Yet past expenditures only predict future expenditures moderately well, and the fact that expenditures rise sharply before death limits persistence, so that many of the high-cost users of Medicare services cannot continue to have high expenditures. We now explore in greater detail the characteristics of high-cost users, particularly those whose high costs extend over more than one year.

Implications for the Long-Term Concentration of Expenditures

We can define persistently high-cost users as beneficiaries whose Medicare expenditures place them in the upper percentiles for multiple years. Table 5.2 displays the characteristics of Medicare recipients who can be considered to have high expenditures over more than one year during our nine-year period of observation. The first row, which shows the percentage of beneficiaries in various categories of persistently high expenditures, suggests that it is unusual for a beneficiary to have multiple years of very high medical expenditures. Over the period, 47% were in the top quintile at some year in the nine-year period. About 30% were in the top decile for one year, but few beneficiaries remained in the top decile for multiple years. For example, only 10% of beneficiaries were in the top decile for two or more years and only 1.2% were in the top decile for four or more of the nine years. Less than 4% were in the top 5% of expenditures for two or more years.

Individuals in high-expenditure categories, especially for multiple years, have very high mortality rates. The two-year mortality rate exceeds 50% for individuals in the top decile for two years or more. It is nearly as high for beneficiaries in the top 20% in two different years. High-cost use in multiple years is associated with greater mortality than very heavy utilization in one year; for example, one- and two-year mortality rates are higher for individuals in the top 20% in any two years than for those in the top 5% in a single year, even though expenditures are much higher in the top 5%. Most deaths occur within one year of the high-cost use (i.e., following the period called "expense sequence" in the table).

Table 5.2
High-cost users of Medicare and their share of expenditures: reimbursements

	Intensity and duration of utilization							
	Top 5% in at least one year	Top 5% in at least two years	Top 10% in at least one year	Top 10% in at least two years	Top 10% in at least three years	Top 20% in at least one year	Top 20% in at least two years	Top 20% in at least three years
Percentage of all beneficiaries	17.1%	3.9%	29.5%	10.0%	3.4%	46.9%	23.0%	11.1%
Percentage who die:								
Within one year of expense sequence	31.1%	37.4%	32.6%	38.3%	40.1%	34.7%	39.8%	41.6%
Within two years of expense sequence	44.0%	53.8%	43.4%	50.6%	53.8%	41.6%	47.4%	49.7%
Percentage in age categories:								
65–69	23.2%	26.7%	24.0%	24.5%	27.2%	15.1%	17.5%	18.9%
70–74	24.3%	25.6%	23.1%	25.3%	26.0%	14.5%	19.4%	22.2%
75–79	22.0%	23.0%	21.2%	21.8%	22.4%	13.3%	17.5%	20.4%
80–84	15.9%	14.5%	16.4%	16.4%	14.6%	10.4%	14.0%	15.6%
85–89	9.9%	7.6%	10.0%	8.9%	8.3%	6.3%	8.3%	9.1%
90–100	4.8%	2.7%	5.4%	3.2%	1.7%	3.3%	3.8%	3.5%
Mean annual reimbursements within percentile group (1996$):								
10th percentile	4,756	9,193	3,203	5,920	8,630	1,743	3,271	4,674
25th percentile	6,593	11,556	4,577	7,527	10,665	2,766	4,509	6,193
50th percentile	9,743	15,120	7,084	10,535	13,738	4,856	6,886	8,794
75th percentile	15,119	20,953	11,777	15,193	18,639	8,785	10,951	12,982
90th percentile	23,439	30,990	18,664	22,617	26,922	14,962	16,910	18,923
Mean annual reimbursements	12,798	18,178	9,769	12,953	16,119	7,259	9,074	10,790
Percentage of total reimbursements group accounts for	58.9%	22.3%	78.1%	41.9%	20.0%	92.5%	66.8%	42.8%

Note: Data are from HCFA (1987–95).

Even though long-term expenditure persistence has a limited extent, the high concentration of expenditures at any given time implies that this small share of beneficiaries may still account for a large portion of long-term Medicare expenditures. The last rows of table 5.2 demonstrate that this is indeed the case. For example, the 30% of beneficiaries in the top decile in any year had average annual expenditures of almost $10,000 over the nine years, and they accounted for 78% of total expenditures during this long period. Similarly, the 3.9% of beneficiaries in the top 5% of expenditures for two or more years accounted for more than one-fifth of Medicare expenditures over the nine year period. These concentrations are considerably lower than a one- or two-year perspective would suggest. For example, beneficiaries in the top decile for one of the nine years have mean expenditures of about $27,000 during that year. Individuals in the top decile for four of the nine years have mean expenditures of more than $29,000 during each of the four years of high expenditures. Although expenditures during a single year are more highly concentrated, these results confirm that a relatively small share of beneficiaries accounts for a large portion of Medicare expenditures over a period of several years.

IV. Discussion

The challenges raised by the existence of a group of patients with predictably high expenditures become greater if those expenditures remain high for prolonged periods. The very fact that a Medicare beneficiary has high expenditures one year, we saw, increases the likelihood that he or she will have high expenditures in a subsequent year. The consequences are many, including the possibility that providers and insurance plans can use information about prior utilization to estimate a potential enrollee's risk of having excessive future expenditures. The challenge is not limited to competitive health insurance or health care markets, either; risk selection at the provider level can occur in any system of regional or national health insurance, whether in the traditional British National Health Service model, a Canadian-style single payor system, or in recently modified versions of these systems that introduce limited capitation at the primary-care physician level and greater financial sensitivity.

Risk selection does not require highly accurate prediction of costs. Any ability to distinguish among groups of patients or beneficiaries expected to have differing average costs is sufficient. Many individuals assigned to a high-cost group could turn out to have below-average costs, and some individuals assigned to low-cost groups subsequently have very high costs. Such group assignment might be inaccurate because only limited relevant information is available or because much of the variation in health costs is truly random. Whatever the reason for the inability to predict health expenditures precisely, adverse selection will occur as long as expected costs can be distinguished.

We analyzed costs over prolonged periods of time among the elderly Medicare population. For the results presented here, we did not use clinical data (such as diagnostic information or previous use of specific procedures) to identify individuals with persistently high costs. But we found that the level of prior utilization, with or without demographic information, strongly predicted future expenses. Heavy use of health services is unlikely to cause heavy use in the future; instead, it is a marker for ill health and other characteristics that lead to consumption of health care. Additional information from the claims files and detailed clinical characteristics would have greatly enhanced our ability to predict expenditures in this population. Most insurers have much more information available in evaluating potential enrollees, and the potential enrollees themselves may know even more about how their health care consumption is likely to deviate from average.

Our major purpose was not to assess predictability, however. We sought to learn whether persistence of high health expenditures is an important phenomenon in the Medicare population. Our results show that it is significant, particularly if we consider the upper quintile of expenditures, but that very few Medicare recipients fall into the top percentiles of expenditures for many years. Thus, the high skewness of expenditures in cross sections of Medicare recipients is not caused by a small group of enrollees who use extraordinary amounts of care year after year. Many of the highest-expenditure beneficiaries die soon thereafter, and many survivors have more modest expenditures in the succeeding years. Individuals who do have persistently high expenditures, however, account for a disproportionately large share of expenditures.

The importance of persistence must be considered in any health care financing reform. For example, financing based on medical savings accounts (MSAs) usually consists of a combination of catastrophic health insurance (i.e., insurance—usually indemnity—with a very high deductible) and a tax-advantaged savings plan to pay for high expenses. Although many of the MSA plans that have been offered by individual employers in the United States have very weak savings features (limited or no ability to carry over unspent funds from one year to the next and no ability to allow returns on balances to accumulate on a tax-deferred basis), the current MSA demonstration and most versions seriously proposed strongly encourage savings. As MSA balances grow large, the funds available for catastrophic deductibles (as well as copayments for the catastrophic insurance component) grow. Whether a given balance is adequate, of course, depends on the level of out-of-pocket expenses an individual bears. These expenses would be high if, for example, an individual approached or reached the catastrophic deductible level for several years. The deductible or catastrophic threshold can be lowered and the copayment rate (or the ceiling on copayments) lowered to provide more insurance and require less reliance on the MSA funds or on non-MSA personal funds.

The features of MSAs allowed for testing under the Health Insurance Portability and Availability Act (HIPAA), which went into effect in 1997, are instructive in this regard. The deductible for qualifying insurance plans is at least $1,500 and no more than $2,250, and the out-of-pocket maximum cannot exceed $3,000. For family accounts, the allowable deductibles range from $3,000 to $4,500 and the out-of-pocket limit is $5,500. An MSA plan directed toward the elderly might feature different deductibles, copayments, or limits than these. But note that the average annual Medicare expenditure exceeds the catastrophic deductible, and that essentially every Medicare recipient with a hospitalization would exceed the deductible that year. Furthermore, our results suggest that many would also reach the ceiling on copayments. If the deductibles and copayments were set so that only the top decile of Medicare recipients would reach the ceiling in any year, about 1% of all beneficiaries would reach the ceiling more than four times over a nine-year period, and nearly a third would reach the ceiling at least once during the nine-year period. For individuals who had contributed to MSAs for decades before reaching these ages, the accumulated funds might readily accommodate such expenses. During a phase-in to MSAs, however, or for individuals who had not been able to build fund balances (for example, because of ongoing medical expenses or inability to make adequate contributions), such expenses might be difficult to bear. The consequences of the moderate degree of persistence in expenditures within the Medicare population depend on the specific features of any MSA plan.

These results are based on a sample of patients whose care was reimbursed on a cost basis (i.e., not on a capitated or "risk" basis). Capitated payments change provider behavior and are expected to modify the amount of care that individuals with persistently high expenses receive. Managed care features might reduce the skewness in expenditures by limiting the amount of care that the highest-cost beneficiaries receive, but this is not certain. For example, the original literature comparing costs of health maintenance organizations (HMOs) and fee-for-service care suggested that HMOs, then the sole example of capitated health care plans, achieved savings by reducing hospitalization rates. Less evidence is available about the costs for hospitalized patients under HMO and fee-for-service plans, but given that a hospitalization has occurred, hospitals treating Medicare patients face incentives very similar to those faced by an HMO. Under PPS, they receive a fixed payment per hospitalization, so there is no incentive to overuse services. In recent years, the routine practice of utilization review and the threat of claims denial have reduced the physicians' and hospitals' discretion to admit patients who could be easily treated on an outpatient basis. For each of these reasons, the growth in Medicare risk contracts, that is, the increased acceptance of capitated payment, may not reduce hospital utilization dramatically, and utilization among Medicare beneficiaries would then remain highly skewed.

If utilization does change, it will be important to learn how it influences outcomes among the sickest Medicare beneficiaries. Our analysis was not designed to assess the appropriateness or effectiveness of expenditures for health care among Medicare recipients. It will be important to learn about their characteristics in much greater clinical detail. We found that individuals with high expenditures have high mortality rates, whether such expenditures are limited to a single year or occur repeatedly. But the majority of patients who reach the top decile of expenditures survive at least two years, and about half the beneficiaries in the top decile for multiple years survive for at least two years. These results clearly show that not all high-cost care is given to individuals who will die soon, reinforcing the concern that dramatic reductions in such care could lead to worsened outcomes among those who now survive after receiving such care. Definitive information about these issues will come only from detailed investigations of the care that severely ill Medicare beneficiaries receive, but these findings suggest that such care cannot be readily dismissed as futile.

References

Ash, Arlene, Frank Porell, Leonard Gruenberg, Eric Sawitz, and Alexa Beiser. 1989. "Adjusting Medicare Capitation Payments Using Prior Hospitalization Data." *Health Care Financing Review* 10(4):17–29.

Berk, Marc L., and Alan C. Monheit. 1992. "The Concentration of Health Expenditures: An Update." *Health Affairs* 11(4):145–9.

Ellis, Randall, Gregory Pope, Lisa Iezzoni, John Ayanian, David Bates, Helen Burstin, and Arlene Ash. 1996. "Diagnosis-Based Risk Adjustment for Medicare Capitation Payments." *Health Care Financing Review* 17(3):101–26.

Enthoven, Alain C., and Sara J. Singer. 1996. "Managed Competition and California's Health Care Economy." *Health Affairs* 15(1):39–57.

Gornick, Marian E., Joan L. Warren, Paul W. Eggers, James D. Lubitz, Nancy DeLew, Margaret H. Davis, and Barbara S. Cooper. 1996. "Thirty Years of Medicare: Impact on the Covered Population." *Health Care Financing Review* 18(2):179–237.

Hoffman, Catherine, Dorothy Rice, and Hai-Yen Sung. 1996. "Persons with Chronic Conditions: Their Prevalence and Costs." *Journal of the American Medical Association* 276(18):1473–9.

Iezzoni, Lisa I., ed. 1994. *Risk Adjustment for Measuring Health Care Outcomes.* Ann Arbor, MI: Health Administration Press.

McClellan, Mark. 1997. "Price and Quality Competition in Health Plan Choice." Stanford University, Stanford, CA. Manuscript.

Pauly, Mark V. 1986. "Taxation, Health Insurance, and Market Failure in the Medical Economy." *Journal of Economic Literature* 24:629–75.

Price, James R., and James W. Mays. 1985. "Selection and the Competitive Standing of Health Plans in a Multiple-Choice, Multiple-Insurer Market." In *Advances in Health Economics and Health Services Research,* eds. Richard M. Scheffler and Louis R. Rossiter, 47–72.

Rothschild, Michael, and Joseph Stiglitz. 1976. "Equilibrium in Competitive Insurance Markets: An Essay on the Economics of Imperfect Information." *Quarterly Journal of Economics* 90:629–50.

Weiner, Jonathan, Allen Dobson, Stephanie Maxwell, Kevin Coleman, Barbara Starfield, and Gerard Anderson. 1996. "Risk-Adjusted Medicare Capitation Rates Using Ambulatory and Inpatient Diagnoses." *Health Care Financing Review* 17(3):77–99.